"Behold the Forest"

"Behold He Prayeth"

By

JOSHUA STAUFFER
*Pastor, Bible Teacher
and Evangelist*

Published by
LIGHT AND HOPE PUBLICATIONS
BERNE, INDIANA

[Printed in the United States of America.]

FOREWORD

Many books have been written on prayer, many sermons preached, and much teaching has been given on this important ministry. However, the half has not been told, nor have many Christians learned the art of earnest, faithful, effective prayer. To do so requires more than the hearing of preaching, the teaching of others, or the reading of writings on prayer. These are helpful, but in order to become efficient in prayer it is essential to read the Bible and obey it, to possess a surrendered will before God and holy desires, to be faithful in regular seasons of daily prayer, and to be led and assisted by the Holy Spirit Who "helpeth our infirmities."

The imperative need of the hour is prayer. A great per cent of those who profess Christianity never pray in public and seldom in secret. If they pray at all, it is a little bedtime prayer. A small number pray, or go through the form, but do so from a sense of duty to ease the conscience. Very few give themselves to prayer, making it their first business in life.

The benefits of prayer are many. Prayer glorifies God, edifies others, and inspires self. This book was born in the secret closet. It was after the writer gave himself more to prayer that these messages came to him. It is hoped that all who read these chapters may catch the inspiration to pray more.

JOSHUA STAUFFER

Westfield, Indiana

TABLE OF CONTENTS

PRAYER

Prayer is the soul's sincere desire,
  Uttered or unexpressed;
The motion of a hidden fire
  That trembles in the breast.

Prayer is the burden of a sigh,
  The falling of a tear,
The upward glancing of an eye
  When none but God is near.

Prayer is the simplest form of speech
  That infant lips can try;
Prayer, the sublimest strains that reach
  The majesty on high.

Prayer is the contrite sinner's voice,
  Returning from his ways;
While angels in their songs rejoice
  And cry, "Behold, he prays!"

Prayer is the Christian's vital breath,
  The Christian's native air,
His watchword at the gate of death;
  He enters heaven with prayer.

O Thou, by Whom we come to God,
  The Life, the Truth, the Way,
The path of prayer Thyself hast trod;
  Lord, teach us how to pray!

James Montgomery

CHAPTER I

"BEHOLD, HE PRAYETH" —(PAUL)

"Behold, he prayeth." These words were spoken by the Lord to one man concerning another man. It is interesting and profitable when reading the Bible to be able to distinguish who the speaker is and to whom the message is given. Sometimes the Father speaks to His Son or to men concerning His Son. Sometimes the Son speaks to the Father, to the Spirit, or to men. Sometimes the Spirit speaks to the Son or to men. Sometimes men speak to God or to men. In the words "Behold, he prayeth," the Lord spoke to Ananias concerning Saul (Paul). What God has to say to men is important, especially that which He has to say to one individual about another. "Behold" means lo, look, see. The Lord became attracted by this man's prayer, then became attached to him. The Lord was looking for a godly man to whom He could tell the good news. "Behold, he prayeth." Who "prayeth"? The man who had been the greatest enemy of the church, who had made havoc of the church, who occasioned the death of Stephen, who had gone forth to arrest the saints, to take them captive, to persecute them! Now, "Behold, he prayeth." How interesting! What greater complimentary statement could the Lord make concerning any man than "Behold, he prayeth"! The spiritual life and ministry of Paul had a blessed commencement, a victorious continuation, and will have a glorious coronation, for he was the man of whom the Lord said, "Behold, he prayeth."

I. He Prayed at His Conversion.

"And he said, Who art Thou, Lord? . . . And he trembling and astonished said, Lord, what wilt Thou have me to do?" (Acts 9: 5, 6).

On his way to Damascus the Lord met Saul and arrested him. He went to arrest others, but instead of arresting the Christians, Christ arrested him. He went to take others captive, but he was captivated by the Lord. He started to Damascus as the greatest enemy of the church and arrived there as the greatest friend of the church. He started as the chiefest of sinners and arrived there as the chiefest of saints. The Lord met and transformed him. After that Saul never was the same. When the Lord met him He flashed a little of His glory on him and said, "Saul, Saul, why persecutest thou Me?" Saul fell to the ground a sinner. He prayed, "Who art Thou, Lord?" Here he was a seeker. He knew this was the voice of the Lord, but as yet he did not know Him as his Lord. The glorified Christ answered, "I am Jesus Whom thou persecutest." This revelation transformed Saul. Now, as a saved, subdued, and submissive man, he prayed, "Lord, what wilt Thou have me to do?" Saul was converted by the direct revelation of the Lord between the time he prayed, "Who art Thou, Lord," (meaning, I do not know Thee, but I want to know Thee) and "Lord, what wilt Thou have me to do?" Saul was born again by the breath of prayer, and on through his life to the end prayer was the spiritual breath of his soul.

II. He Prayed at His Baptism with the Spirit.

"And the Lord said unto him, Arise, and go into the street which is called Straight, and enquire in the house of Judas for one called Saul, of Tarsus: for, behold, he prayeth" (Acts 9:11).

"And Ananias went his way, and entered into the house; and putting his hands on him said, Brother Saul, the Lord, even Jesus, that appeared unto thee in the way as thou camest, hath sent me, that thou mightest receive thy sight, and be filled with the Holy Ghost" (Acts 9:17).

Saul needed another Christian experience wrought in his life to qualify him to enter into the ministry. He had been converted on the way to Damascus by the direct revelation of Christ, as one born out of due time. He needed to be baptized with the Holy Ghost for cleansing and enduement. He was blind for three days, during which time he neither ate nor drank, but he did much thinking and praying. As Ananias came in and laid his hands on him, he addressed him as "Brother," acknowledging the Lord's revelation to him on the way. He acknowledged him as a brother in the Lord and fellowshiped him. Through the ministry of Ananias, Saul received his sight and was filled with the Holy Ghost. Saul went forth a praying man, and a fitting epithet from then on to the end of his ministry would be "Behold, he prayeth."

III. He Prayed During His Ministry.

"And when they had ordained them elders in every church, and had prayed with fastings, they commended them to the Lord, on Whom they believed" (Acts 14:23).

Prayer with fastings involves time. From this Scripture we get an inkling, or an insight, into Paul's prayer life. From the tenor of Paul's writings, his admonition to the churches, and the pastoral Epistles, we conclude that he prayed much for the success of his ministry. This was the great secret of his success. Well may every minister take this to heart and do likewise.

IV. He Prayed in His Evangelistic Campaigns.

"And on the sabbath we went out of the city by a river side, where prayer was wont to be made" (Acts 16:13).

An evangelist should pray much, because of the importance of his ministry and the benefits prayer will have on his evangelistic labors. As a rule, while he is engaged in an evangelistic campaign he has little to do but preach and pray, and, therefore, he should do much praying, because of the need and the time afforded him to pray. Paul has left us an example along this line. While he was waiting for the occasion to come for preaching he resorted to the river side where prayer was offered to the Lord. Blessed will be the evangelist who prays much, who keeps prayed up-to-date between revival meetings and during revivals, and does not need to spend several days praying to catch up with the church or get revived himself before he becomes useful to sinners.

V. He Prayed in His Tribulation.

"And at midnight Paul and Silas prayed, and sang praises unto God: and the prisoners heard them" (Acts 16:25).

Paul, unlike many who are cast into prison who plot and plan how to get out or how to get even with civil authorities, prayed and sang praises to God. His back was sore and bleeding from the beating he received. Sleep was impossible. Therefore, he spent the time praying for his enemies and in singing praises to God. He did not turn sour or become bitter, but retained the blessing of God on his soul.

VI. He Prayed in His Daily Duties.

"For God is my witness, Whom I serve with my spirit in the gospel of His Son, that without ceasing I make mention of you always in my prayers" (Rom. 1:9).

"Wherefore I also, after I heard of your faith in the Lord Jesus, and love unto all the saints, cease not to give thanks for you, making mention of you in my prayers" (Eph. 1:15, 16).

Many people pray only in time of need or distress. The person who is regular and faithful in praying daily will be heard by the Lord. Such a person was Paul. He did not confine his prayers on himself, but he prayed daily for the churches he established and the converts he made. Paul also saturated his prayers with thanksgiving unto God for the people for whom he prayed. This made his prayers effective before God. The motto of his daily life was "Behold, he prayeth."

VII. He Prayed When in Peril.

"For there stood by me this night the angel of God, Whose I am, and Whom I serve, saying, Fear not, Paul . . . And when he had thus spoken, he took bread, and gave thanks to God in the presence of them all: and when he had broken it, he began to eat. Then were they all of good cheer, and they also took some meat" (Acts 27:23, 24, 35, 36).

By reading the twenty-seventh chapter of Acts we receive an insight into the inner life and conduct in time of peril of the man of whom the Lord said, "Behold, he prayeth." He prayed not only for himself but for every one on the ship. Every one on board was blessed because Paul was on board, and all owed their lives to Paul and his prayers. Such is the value of a man of prayer.

If the Lord would behold many people, what would He see? If the predominating thing in their lives were recorded, it simply would be, "Behold, he sleepeth;" or "Behold, he readeth the newspaper;" or "Behold, he listeneth to the radio;" or "Behold, he smoketh;" or "Behold, he playeth;" or "Behold, she cooketh;" or "Behold, she seweth;" or "Behold, she talketh." But of the person who makes prayer the first, greatest, and most important business in life, God and heaven will take notice that "Behold, he prayeth." May this be said of you.

CHAPTER II

PRAYER DEFINED

Prayer is more than saying words. Words which are supposed to be prayer may not always be prayer. Whenever we attempt to pray to the Lord, He does not merely listen to the words, but He looks into the heart of the pray-er. From the Scriptures we learn that true prayer is a combination of bowing the soul before God, pouring out the heart to God, lifting up the soul unto God, looking to God in expectancy, seeking the face and favor of God, calling on His name, and making known our supplication to Him.

Our prayers should be offered intelligently to the Lord. The desires and thoughts should be expressed in words to Him. The Lord, through the prophet Hosea, spoke to Israel, saying, "Take with you words, and turn to the Lord: say unto Him, Take away all iniquity, and receive us graciously: so will we render the calves of our lips" (Hosea 14:2). Here the Lord puts words, a prayer and a confession, in the lips of Israel so they will know what to say.

Prayer is asking—talking to God, making our requests known to Him. The following Scriptures teach that prayer is asking:

"Ask, and it shall be given you; seek, and ye shall find; knock, and it shall be opened unto you" (Matt. 7:7).

"For every one that asketh receiveth; and he that seeketh findeth; and to him that knocketh it shall be opened" (Matt. 7:8).

"If ye then, being evil, know how to give good gifts unto your children, how much more shall your Father which is in heaven give good things to them that ask Him?" (Matt. 7:11).

"If ye shall ask any thing in My name, I will do it" (John 14:14).

"If ye abide in Me, and My words abide in you, ye shall ask what ye will, and it shall be done unto you" (John 15:7).

"Hitherto have ye asked nothing in My name: ask, and ye

shall receive, that your joy may be full" (John 16:24).

With the asking there need to be holy desires, spiritual feelings, earnest expressions, and taking righteous attitudes before God.

I. Prayer is Bowing the Soul and Knees Before God.

"For this cause I bow my knees unto the Father of our Lord Jesus Christ" (Eph. 3:14).

Bowing the knees before God is a good act, and an attitude of prayer, faith, and worship. The mere bowing is not prayer, but when it is before God with the object of receiving from Him, it becomes an element of prayer. Praying is an act vastly more than that of saying words. God considers the attitude of our outward being, of the inner man—the feelings, motives, love in the heart, desires, faith in Him, and the words which are in our mouths, or in our thoughts, when we pray. The act and attitude of getting low before God is taking the right attitude before Him. When the soul bows before Him, He will stoop low to analyze the desires of the heart, to hear what we have to say; and He will also lift us up.

II. Prayer is Pouring Out the Heart to God

"And Hannah answered and said, No, my lord, I am a woman of a sorrowful spirit: I have drunk neither wine nor strong drink, but have poured out my soul before the Lord" (I Sam. 1:15).

"Trust in Him at all times; ye people, pour out your heart before Him" (Ps. 62:8).

Here is another element of prayer. Pouring out the heart to God is an act of self-emptying. This makes room for God. The inward feelings, burdens, and desires of the heart of a saint of God can not be adequately expressed in words. When these holy desires and feelings are poured out to God, they are cast before Him even as the contents of a bucket are all poured out at the feet of a rich and capable benefactor who then fills the empty vessel with his bounties. The pouring out of holy longings to the Lord, whether by words, urgings, will, groanings, or otherwise, will be accepted by the Lord as a sacrifice to Him. Doing so

makes room for God, and in return He gives us His
benefits, blessings, and favors. Such a pouring out of
the heart is mentioned in the text concerning Hannah,
which was something vastly more than words, and came
from a deeper source than the lips.

III. Prayer is Lifting Up the Soul unto God
"Unto Thee, O Lord, do I lift up my soul" (Ps. 25:1).
"Let us lift up our heart with our hands unto God in the
heavens" (Lam. 3:41).

The soul, which expresses the spiritual life, feelings
and will, can be lifted up to God. This inward longing
may express itself in sighs or inward groanings. The
soul that bows itself low before the Lord can then lift
itself up unto God. Of course, there must be an utter
abandonment unto God and a full surrender before the
Spirit of God will inspire an inward and upward urge
which draws the heart to God.

IV. Prayer is Looking Up to God in Expectancy
"My voice shalt Thou hear in the morning, O Lord; in the
morning will I direct my prayer unto Thee, and will look up"
(Ps. 5:3).

Praying is similar to the shooting of an arrow. The
bow is faith; the arrow is the petition; and the mark
is the throne of grace. The person who shoots an arrow
does so with the objective of hitting a mark. When an
arrow is shot, the archer observes whether he has hit
the mark. Looking up to God with an expectancy is an
act of prayer and faith. This eliminates the hurry-up
spirit while we are praying. After David had prayed,
he looked up to see what reaction his prayer had made.
The face expresses much, even approval or disapproval.
David expected to see God's approval, which to him
meant that the Lord would grant his petition.

V. Prayer is Seeking the Face and Favor of God
"When Thou saidst, Seek ye My face; my heart said unto
Thee, Thy face, Lord, will I seek" (Ps. 27:8).

The marginal rendering of this verse is: "My heart
said unto Thee, Let my face seek Thy face." Seeking the
face of a person is getting his attention. Then when

our eyes are fixed upon his eyes, and his eyes meet our eyes, we have obtained recognition. Praying is looking directly as it were into the face of God and attracting His attention; and when eyes meet, we know He has heard. The approval of His face means He will grant our petitions. It is only as we take cognizance of Him and as He takes cognizance of us, or as we give Him our attention and He gives us His attention, that our prayers will be answered.

VI. Prayer is Calling upon the Name of the Lord

"And there he builded an altar unto the Lord, and called upon the name of the Lord" (Gen. 12:8).

"Then called I upon the name of the Lord; O Lord, I beseech Thee, deliver my soul" (Ps. 116:4).

Prayer is coming to God, even into His presence by faith, which is approaching the throne of grace, and there bowing at His feet, calling upon Him. There are several manners of address given in the Bible, such as, "God," "O Lord," "Lord God," "Our Father," "Heavenly Father," "O righteous Father," etc. This may seem of little importance, yet it reveals to some degree our spiritual state. The sinner has no claim on Deity only as "God," or "Savior." The Christian who always addresses Deity as "God" or "O God," needs to learn a closer and dearer relation, even that of "Father," and he as a son.

VII. Prayer is Making Supplication to God

"Make thy supplication to the Almighty" (Job 8:5).

"And I set my face unto the Lord God, to seek by prayer and supplications, with fasting, and sackcloth, and ashes: And I prayed unto the Lord my God" (Dan. 9:3, 4).

To supplicate is to make a humble entreaty, or an earnest petition, to God. Prayer is the language of want, and of asking. This asking may express itself in repetitions. Repetitions, if earnest and fervent, are good, and are practiced more or less by all great men of prayer. The Bible condemns "vain repetitions" when praying. The repetition in asking for a good thing is not vain. In Gethsemane Christ prayed three times for the same thing. Elijah prayed seven times for rain. David, Daniel, and Paul prayed again and again for the same things.

CHAPTER III

ACCOMPANIMENTS OF PRAYER

Praying is not the asking for anything and everything we want without giving our wants some considerations and also God's glory. Neither can we do as we please and obtain from God everything we want. There are some concomitants of prayer. These should be considered carefully by all who would be efficient in praying, for they will aid faith, inspire the prayer and help it to go through and touch the throne of grace. On the divine side the concomitants will have a great weight in influencing God to hearken. Seven concomitants are mentioned. In some cases doing one or several of these things will be a great aid in getting our prayers through. These should be considered carefully to observe which one, or ones, will be helpful in prayer.

I. Repentance.

"When Thy people Israel be smitten down before the enemy, because they have sinned against Thee, and shall turn again to Thee, and confess Thy name, and pray, and make supplication unto Thee in this house: Then hear Thou in heaven, and forgive the sin of Thy people Israel, and bring them again unto the land which Thou gavest unto their fathers" (I Kings 8: 33, 34).

Repentance is an essential element in obtaining salvation. The sinner who repents of his sins will obtain mercy from the Lord. Repentance means a change of mind, a change of purpose, a godly sorrow for sins or for failures. God is so loving, patient, and merciful that His loving heart is easily touched. When the sinner repents, God will have mercy on Him.

We think that only sinners need to repent, but this applies to God's people also, because there may be failure, departure, and shortcomings on the part of

many people. One of the greatest saints of the last
generation, who has been greatly used by the Lord in
awakening many in two continents, said that he repented a thousand times more after he was converted
than he did in getting converted. On the part of many
there may be failure or secret sins. Coming before the
Lord with a deep contrition of heart will move Him to
hear the cry of any one in prayer.

It would be good for many Christian people to repent frequently in the sense of changing their minds, or
in changing their purposes. It is possible for good people to have their minds and hearts set about some
things which they loathe to change, even if a better
way may be suggested by others. Some may have a
personal or selfish purpose concerning some things. If
this is so, it would be a great aid in getting God to answer their prayers if they would repent along those
lines.

II. Confession

"And I prayed unto the Lord my God, and made my confession, . . . We have sinned, and have committed iniquity, and
have done wickedly, and have rebelled, even by departing from
Thy precepts and from Thy judgments" (Dan. 9:4, 5).

Confession is another element which moves God.
The sinner who will confess his sins before the Lord is
promised forgiveness. To confess to the Lord is to hide
nothing from Him, but to unbosom all that is not good
before Him. It is a sin and folly to try to hide things
from the Lord, for He knows all about us any way. To
do so shows a love for things that He hates.

When sick people who are sinners seek healing,
confess their sins and seek Christ as their Savior, their
confession and prayer will be heard, and the Lord will
freely forgive their sins. Then, as a rule healing will
come freely and easily. When a Christian is sick and
his sickness has come as a chastisement from the Lord,
or if he has failed along some line, a confession to the
Lord or to others is the condition which will move God
to answer prayer. James gives some good instruction,

which is the scriptural course afflicted and sick people should follow. "Is any among you afflicted? let him pray. Is any merry? let him sing psalms. Is any sick among you? let him call for the elders of the church; and let them pray over him, anointing him with oil in the name of the Lord: and the prayer of faith shall save the sick, and the Lord shall raise him up; and if he have committed sins, they shall be forgiven him. Confess your faults one to another, and pray one for another, that ye may be healed. The effectual fervent prayer of a righteous man availeth much" (James 5:13-16).

When there are faults—and all people have them, failures, a lack in prayer, in reading the Bible or in being fervent for the Lord, any unkindness or a lack of wisdom in dealing with others, the utterance of hasty or unkind words, faultfinding, evil habits, worldliness, a love for worldly books and magazines and pictures, the resorting to worldly places and anything that displeases the Lord; when these are confessed and forsaken, God will answer prayer. An honest confession is good for the soul, will lift a great load, will restore confidence, and will let much of heaven come in on the scene. Whenever prayers are not answered, a self-examination should be made to see whether confession needs to be made.

III. Self-abasement

"And Abraham answered and said, Behold now, I have taken upon me to speak unto the Lord, which am but dust and ashes" (Gen. 18:27).

Getting low before the Lord and humbling self before Him moves Him to give attention to our prayers. It is when we get low before the Lord that we touch the arm that is beneath us. God's right arm, His everlasting arm, is beneath us; His left arm, His mighty hand, is over us; and we are between. He employs the hand we touch. Peter admonishes us to submit ourselves under the mighty hand of God which is over us; then in due season He would exalt us. His hand which is above us will be employed to humble us when we go so high in self-exaltation as to touch it. When in humiliation we get low before Him and touch the arm that is under us, that hand will bear us up. When we exalt ourselves, it will be disgusting to others and nauseating to self; but when God exalts us, it will be edifying to others and gratifying to self. Every Christian should live in humility continually, especially when he desires God to hear and answer his prayers, for that is a good time to get low before the Lord and recognize Him as almighty, and we, like Abraham, as being but dust and ashes. This moves God to give attention to our prayers.

IV. Weeping

"They shall come with weeping, and with supplications will I lead them" (Jer. 31:9).

There is a language in tears. An infant has no language but that of a cry. A wise mother will soon understand the meaning of the cry of her child, whether it is a cry of pain, hunger, or anger. There are different kinds of tears. The Lord understands our tears. Tears should be the expression of an inward tender feeling which can not be expressed in words. When in communion with God there are inward yearnings which we cannot express to the Lord in words; but we can express them in tears, and those tears move the Lord to give attention to our prayers. The Lord sees our tears as well as He hears our cry. There is power in tears if they are of the right type, and are shed for the right purpose. Such tears are an aid to prayer.

V. Fasting

"And it came to pass, when I heard these words, that I sat down and wept, and mourned certain days, and fasted, and prayed before the God of heaven" (Neh. 1:4).

"And when they had fasted and prayed, and laid their hands on them, they sent them away" (Acts 13:3).

Fasting is an aid to prayer. It moves God, and is good for the saint who is engaged in prayer. Fasting is recommended in the Bible. It is of importance in the success of intercession. It pleases the Lord when it is done with a right motive. Its benefits are twofold, even negative and positive. Its negative purposes are: it allows more time for prayer; it allows more clearness of mind, for when the stomach is full a person cannot be at his best in praying; it leads to a more definite purpose in praying; and it leads from the natural to the spiritual. The objective virtues are: it pleases God; God honors it; and God blesses the spirit of self-denial. Fasting and prayer go together well.

VI. Watchfulness

"But the end of all things is at hand: be ye therefore sober, and watch unto prayer" (I Peter 4: 7).

On several occasions Christ commanded His disciples to "Watch and pray." Christ not only commanded His disciples to watch, but He said, "What I say unto you, I say unto all, Watch." The term "watch" is employed in the New Testament generally in connection with the end of the age, or Christ's second coming, and with prayer. Sobriety and watchfulness also go together. Great care needs to be exercised by the Christian that he conduct himself wisely, that the temper of his mind be grave, fixed, and solid, that a strict observance be maintained in being temperate in the enjoyment of earthly enjoyments, that the enemy does not gain an entrance, that he will "watch unto prayer," that is, be in a sober state, fit for prayer, and to be instant and frequent in prayer.

VII. Praise and Thanksgiving

"I cried unto Him with my mouth, and He was extolled with my tongue" (Ps. 66: 17).

"Be careful for nothing; but in everything by prayer and supplication with thanksgiving let your requests be made known unto God" (Phil. 4: 6).

It is well to saturate our prayers with praise. We have heard it expressed again and again that "Prayer changes things." It also can be said, "Praise changes things." If we have prayed and no answer has come, we should try praising God for the thing we have asked. Paul was a man of prayer. It is interesting to observe in his writings that his prayers are full of praise. Prayer and praise are a splendid combination. They are like the two wings of a bird. A bird could not soar up with only one wing, but when two wings are employed, that will bear it up. Many people do not employ the wing of praise enough in their prayers. Their lives are lived on a low plane. They can not soar above some trials in life. David obtained many answers to prayer, and accomplished much for the Lord. He not only prayed much, but he praised the Lord much. He was the Master of Thanksgiving in the Old Testament. Paul obtained many answers to prayer, and he too praised the Lord much, and for everything. He was the Master of Thanksgiving (M.T) of the New Testament. Practice praising God more, for it will have a most wholesome effect in your prayer life.

CHAPTER IV

POSTURES IN PRAYER

The posture in prayer seems to be a minor matter; however, it is of greater importance than we at first may realize. The Bible reveals different postures of men during periods of prayer. These different postures should be considered, for there will be spiritual benefit in doing so. Some people become prejudiced against certain postures in prayer. Some people kneel when a leader says, "Let us stand for prayer." Others will remain seated when all are asked to kneel, or some will remain seated when all are asked to stand. A safe rule to follow is to keep the unity of the Spirit and the service, and do as the pastor, or leader, suggests. Different postures may be profitable on different occasions and in different places. In this the minister should lead wisely. It may be well in a tent meeting, especially when it is damp, to request the congregation to stand while prayer is offered, and in a street meeting, or when there is a large congregation and people are crowded. A congested audience can not kneel with comfort. This is true where the benches are too close together. There should be ample room between the benches to allow worshipers to kneel with comfort, or to allow a personal worker to enter, or for a seeker to step out to go forward to seek the Lord. The closeness of benches has been the means of defeat again and again. Then there are many who are getting away from kneeling altogether. As a rule kneeling is one of the most practical postures to take, especially for a continued season of prayer, on prayer meeting night, or when it is well to prostrate self before the Lord. The feelings and attitudes of the inner man give expression through the outer man. The outward conduct and actions are an index to the state of the inner man. It is well to remember that there are times when the outer man needs to lead in taking the right attitude before the Lord to bring the inner man to the same state. Let us consider the Bible teaching on the posture to take before the Lord.

I. Standing

"And Solomon stood before the altar of the Lord in the presence of all the congregation of Israel, and spread forth his hands toward heaven" (I Kings 8:22).

"And when ye stand praying, forgive, if ye have ought against any: that your Father also which is in heaven may forgive you your trespasses" (Mark 11:25).

Standing is not an improper posture for prayer. It was generally practiced by the Jews. It is claimed that the Jews called their prayers their standing. The Bible endorses standing as a posture to take when offering prayer to God, and there are occasions when standing is very appropriate. Solomon stood to pray at the dedication of the temple. Abraham stood before the Lord as he interceded for the righteous in Sodom. Abraham's servant stood by the well of water as he prayed for the right damsel to come along which should become the bride of Isaac. Moses stood before the Lord on the mount while the Lord appeared to him. Hannah stood while she prayed for a son. In giving instruction on prayer Christ said, "When ye stand praying." He did not mean that standing was the only proper attitude to take while praying. The Lord hears our prayers as we stand before Him when they are offered in humility and faith.

II. Bowing Down

"O come, let us worship and bow down: let us kneel before the Lord our Maker" (Ps. 95:6).

Bowing the head, when it is before the Lord, is an attitude of worship and reveals respect to God. Every time any one appears before the Lord in prayer he should reverence God. This may be done standing, sitting, or kneeling. We should ever bear in mind, whenever we appear before the Lord in prayer, that He looks into the heart and considers the state more than He does the posture; however, bowing the head is one good posture to take before the Lord when engaged in prayer, or when another prays.

III. Kneeling

"And when he had thus spoken, he kneeled down, and prayed with them all" (Acts 20:36).

Under ordinary circumstances kneeling should be the predominating posture to assume in a season of prayer. The early Christians used this humble and reverent gesture of kneeling, especially on the days they fasted. It has the advantage of humility in form. Humility is an essential accompaniment to effective praying. Man was fearfully and wonderfully made. God made him so that he could kneel and take the posture of surrender, submission, and humility when engaged in prayer and worship. Kneeling is mentioned, or intimated, as a posture over ten times in the Bible. Let it be remembered that it is not the only proper attitude to assume when praying.

IV. Falling on the Face

"And He went a little farther, and fell on His face, and prayed" (Matt. 26:39).

Lying on the face in a prostrate form before the Lord is getting as low before Him as possible in a bodily posture. The attitude we take before the Lord has much to do with moving Him. When any person gets low before Him, that moves Him to condescend to meet the worshiper. During great distress, agony, or dire need it is proper to lie prostrate before the Lord. Job in his great grief fell on the ground. The Jews expressed great grief by rolling in the dust. Christ lying prostrate on the ground revealed His submission, humility, and reverential fear. It is well to assume this attitude before the Lord. Contrition and humility greatly move the Lord. He said, "I dwell in the high and holy place, with him also that is of a contrite and humble spirit, to revive the spirit of the humble, and to revive the heart of the contrite ones" (Isa. 57:15). Before we can meet Him in the habitation of His high and holy place, He must meet us in the low place of contrition and humiliation. This is the place that the Eternal One will meet us at any time.

V. Lying Down

"Then Hezekiah turned his face toward the wall, and prayed unto the Lord" (Isa. 38:2).

Hezekiah was lying on a bed when he prayed for his healing. Many saints have prayed while lying down in time of affliction or while resting. Many more have prayed in hours of wakefulness when sleep departed from them. In fact, it is a good thing to pray when sleep has departed. While lying down is a good time to hear from the Lord. He has spoken to many people in dreams, in visions, in a still small voice in the night hours.

VI. Looking Up with Open Eyes

"My voice shalt Thou hear in the morning, O Lord; in the morning will I direct my prayer unto Thee, and will look up" (Ps. 5:3).

"And He commanded the multitude to sit down on the grass, and took the five loaves, and the two fishes, and looking up to heaven, He blessed, and brake, and gave the loaves to His disciples" (Matt. 14:19).

Most people make it a practice to close their eyes during prayer. This has its virtues while praying in public. It aids concentration and prevents mind wanderings. However, when alone or in public it is scriptural to look up, and with open eyes offer prayer to the Lord. This example was practiced by a number of saints in the Bible. In fact, Christ practiced this when He prayed. His looking up to heaven teaches us to look to God as our Father Who is in heaven and from Whom all blessings flow.

VII. Lifting Up and Spreading Forth Holy Hands

"I will therefore that men pray every where, lifting up holy hands, without wrath and doubting" (I Tim. 2:8).

The lifting and spreading forth of the hands has

been the attitude of many people in seasons of prayer. It expresses a state of surrender, of submission, of taking our hands off, and even a desire for God to take things into His hands. The hands of Jochebed pitched the ark with pitch within and without, placed Moses within, then pushed him out in the river among the flags. Jochebed then took her hands off. She could pray with holy, uplifted hands which were soiled with pitch; and though they were black, yet they were holy hands. It was then that God took matters in hand. Hannah led Samuel to Eli and left him before the Lord. She took her hands off and left him in the hands of the Lord. The lifting up of holy hands is expressive of holy doings. The Lord considers what we have been doing when we pray. If we can show Him holy hands, it will help to get our prayers through. It is well to bear in mind that God hears prayer when it is offered to Him in faith and humility, as we kneel, stand, bow, sit, walk, ride, or lie down. It is a good policy at times to break the monotony and change the form, for God delights in variety.

CHAPTER V

THE TIME ELEMENT IN PRAYER

God fills all time and all space. He can perform things instantly, or He can spread His providence over extended periods of time. Man is a creature of time and fills but little of it, and only a little space. He is allotted only a limited period of time in which to accomplish his life's work. It requires time for man to do things, to serve the Lord, to be holy, and to pray. Time does not make men holy, but it is an essential element which must enter into our prayers, and in worshiping God. It takes time to grow spiritually and to reach maturity, even as it does to grow physically. Time comes from God for it is He Who gives it to us, and He has commanded us to redeem it because the days are evil. He expects us to spend some of it in prayer. Doing so will redeem it and invest it wisely, which will glorify God, bless others, and benefit us in time and in eternity.

I. True Prayer Requires Time

Rushing into the place of prayer, being in a hurry to get started, crowding the prayer to get through and to get out again in order to do something else, is not true praying. Such a spirit is a great hindrance to prayer. The earnest effectual prayer of a righteous man will cost him something. One thing which man must sacrifice to offer prayer is time. If our prayers are offered unto God without any sacrifice or cost to us, they will not move God greatly, nor court His favor, neither result in a gracious answer. Our prayers should be offered unto God; that is, we should put something into them which is of cost to us, such as time, fervency, and a soul agony. Offered means given up, given with a price, even with some sacrifice on our part. If our service does not cost us anything, it is cheap service. If our prayers do not cost us anything, they are cheap prayers. It is possible for people to come to God to pray in the same spirit that they go to a store to purchase things. They want to buy the best goods and materials for a small sum, and even then pay for them very reluctantly. People want to receive much from God, yet desire to get it by offering little unto Him. The blessings of God can not be purchased, but they are obtained by meeting the divine requirements. The time element figures in life, and labors, but especially in our prayers. Let us sacrifice time freely and joyfully, and spend much of it in prayer.

II. True Prayer Eliminates the Hurry-up Spirit

The great word of the world is "hurry," but the great word in the Bible, in Christian experience, and in a successful ministry for the Lord is the word "wait." A hurry-up spirit is not of God. He gives us sufficient time to do His will. Satan would keep us from praying at all if he can; and when he can not do that, he would have us pray but a brief time, do it in a "hurry-up" spirit, and rush us through with as little time spent in prayer as possible. A person is not in a right attitude to pray efficiently unto God while he is possessed with a "hurry-up" spirit. Not only does it take time to pray, but often it takes time to get into a spirit of prayer. Meditation is an essential element and accompaniment of prayer. It requires time to meditate. Meditation is becoming a lost art to many people. We are commanded many times in the Scriptures to meditate. The Lord would draw us aside and get us to give up everything to meditate on Him. God Himself has said, "Be still and know that I am God." If we want to become acquainted with God, we must be still before Him. Time should be taken when we enter into the secret closet until the "hurry-up" spirit is eliminated and the heart has meditated upon God and become silent in His presence. We can not take the attitude a woman did in a prayer meeting. She endured it instead of enjoying it; then when it was all over gave a sigh of relief and said, "Well, thank God, this is now over for another week." When a like attitude is taken in prayer and we rejoice because the season is over, such praying will not receive great answers.

III. True Prayer Requires a Heart Preparation

It is essential before we pray to get into a spirit of prayer. Frequently the Holy Spirit prepares us for the secret closet. When such is not the case we should wait for a concern, for a spirit of prayer, and for a divine fervency. Time should be taken until these come to us and warm our hearts to prepare us to pray. It is a sin before God and a mockery to Him to rush into the place of prayer, crowd our prayers through, then forget what we have asked. A heart preparation is necessary for prayer. Taking time, meditating, being still to become conscious of God and His presence, with submission and humility, prepare the heart for praying. When this preparation has come and all conditions are met, God will be pleased, and we may come boldly to the throne of grace and importune in prayer.

When we are careless in our asking and there has been no meditation, no waiting on God, no consideration as to what we should ask, no heart desire, no sacrifice in offering the prayer, no soul passion, there will be no faith, no hope, no results, and no answer. When we pray God does not merely listen to our words, our voice, and our pleadings, but He looks deeper than the vocal cords, from which come the words and voice, even into our hearts and the doings of our hands. When He sees that we have pure hearts (holy hearts) and clean hands (righteous doings), He will give our prayers His consideration. Some years ago a splendid cartoon appeared in print. It was that of a woman kneeling and praying unto God with her face and hands uplifted. Out of her mouth came the words, "Yes, Lord; Yes, Lord." God was not looking at her words nor into her mouth, but into her heart. In her heart there was a large black "No." This woman lacked a heart preparation and was not ready to pray; neither was God ready to answer her prayer.

IV. True Prayer May Demand Fastings and Wrestlings

Many times Satan will contest the case of a saint of God. He will put up a tremendous struggle to prevent him from praying, to hinder him in his praying, and to keep the prayer from going through. Then on the other hand Satan would prevent the answer from coming back to the saint. Between the Christian on earth and Christ on the throne of grace in heaven Satan has his seat of power, in which are located all of his hosts and forces. When the Christian prays, his prayers must break through this host of wickedness. Sometimes the answer is delayed. It is then that the Christian must hold on to God in wrestlings and sometimes in fastings, that is, in giving up the physical necessities in order to give more time to prayer and to be in a better condition to pray. An example of this fact was that of Daniel who prayed for twenty-one days before the answer came. When we come to the place that we want the answer more than we want food, or pleasure, or ease, or anything else, and we sacrifice time and meals, such praying will prevail with God and defeat the enemy. God will honor it, and answer such earnest praying.

V. True Prayer Should Be Long in Secret

One of the great dangers of secret praying is that we do not pray long enough. There is no virtue in long prayers being offered merely for the sake of praying a long time; however, the place to pray long is in secret. The mistake many people make is that they pray little, or not at all, in secret. Then when they do pray in public, they seem to make up for it, hold on, and take too much time. Such a spirit kills the spiritual influence of a service.

Christ prayed long in secret—sometimes all night. The seventeenth chapter of John is the longest recorded prayer of Christ. There may be rare cases in which

long prayers may be offered in public, that is, when the
Holy Spirit comes on a person to do so. When the Spirit
moves a person to pray long in public, he will recognize
it, and so will everyone else in his presence. When such
an occasion comes, the offerer should hold on and
plead with God, keeping it up as long as the Spirit im-
presses him. Then everyone else should fall in line and
join in the spirit of the prayer. If an all day meeting or
an all night prayer meeting is scheduled, it is appropriate to offer longer prayers, but even then it is well to
have periods of silence and meditation, confession and
praise.

The virtue of lingering in the presence of God until
a heart preparation comes to pray, and of continuing in
prayer is the worshiper becomes like God, and His
image becomes stamped on him. It was while Moses
lingered long in the presence of God that he imbibed
His holiness, which caused his face to shine when he
came down from the mount. Mary of Bethany frequently lingered at the feet of Jesus, and it was there
that she learned of Him and became like her Master.

VI. True Prayer May Be Short in Public

Some people condemn short prayers and make fun
of them. The virtue of praying does not consist in long
prayers, neither in short prayers, but rather in fervent
prayers. It is neither long prayers nor short prayers
that move God, but the earnest desire, the fervency of
spirit, and faith that move God to answer. God looks on
the heart—its purity, motives, desires, and faith—when
He listens to our prayers. Short prayers are more
adapted for the public. Those who pray much in secret
do not need to pray so long in public. It is an art to
know how to pray in public, to pray for the need of the
hour, to pray for the needs of the people in our presence,
and to be specific. This pleases the Lord much more
than to pray around the world, to exhort and preach
while praying, and to make the prayer too general.
Elijah on Mount Carmel was prepared for the occasion

because he had spent much time in secret, praying during the three and one-half years of the drought and famine. The Baal worshipers prayed for several hours very frantically to their gods, but no fire fell. When Elijah's time came, he prepared his sacrifice and offered a prayer of sixty-three words, which required only forty seconds to offer, then the fire fell. He was prayed up-to-date and didn't need to pray long in public. Christ at the tomb of Lazarus offered a short prayer of forty words, which required only thirty seconds to offer. He too had prayed through in secret concerning the raising of Lazarus from the dead before He arrived. In His prayer He said, "Father, I thank Thee that Thou hast heard Me." From this we learn that He had prayed through concerning Lazarus before He arrived at Bethany; therefore, a short prayer was all that needed to be offered in public. In the cases of Elijah and Christ it was far more pleasing to God and impressive to the people that prayer should be answered suddenly by short, positive petitions. Should either have had to pray a long drawn out prayer in public, it would not have been as impressive to the people nor glorified God as much. When Peter was sinking on the sea, he did not offer a long dry prayer, such as some people do in public, before they come to the object of their asking; for if he had, he would have been at the bottom of the sea long before he came to the place of saying, "Lord, save me." Peter's prayer was short, positive, and direct. All public praying, unless the Lord leads otherwise, should be short and positive.

VII. Examples of Men Who Took Time to Pray

All great men in the ministry have been men of prayer. David made it a practice to pray three times daily, and so did Daniel. Christ was a man of great prayer Who prayed much in secret. The apostle Peter was a man of prayer. In the writings of the New Testament we get a glimpse into the hidden life of Peter, from which we learn that he spent much time in prayer. He, with John, went to the temple at the hour of prayer;

then at the house of Simon the tanner, in Joppa, we learn he spent a part of a day on the house top praying. Paul also spent much time in prayer. John Wesley spent two hours daily in prayer; arising every morning at four o'clock, he prayed until six. He made prayer the greatest business of his life. John Fletcher often prayed all night and stained his walls with prayer, and the heavens too. Martin Luther spent from two to three hours in prayer every day. He said, "If I fail to spend two hours in prayer each morning, the Devil gets the victory through the day. I have so much business I can not get on without spending three hours daily in prayer." Samuel Rutherford possessed a heavenly fragrance; and this was given unto him because he arose at three o'clock in the morning to meet God. All great men in the ministry became great because they prayed much in secret. No doubt many more men might have been great if they had prayed more.

CHAPTER VI

FRUITS OF A PRAYERFUL LIFE

"Therefore I say unto you, What things soever ye desire, when ye pray, believe that ye receive them, and ye shall have them" (Mark 11:24).

God has ordained that everything shall increase, and bring forth after its kind. Above all other things the Christian should bring forth after his kind. There are two kinds of fruit every Christian should bear, the fruit of "being" and the fruit of "doing." The fruit of "being" is called "the fruit of the Spirit." The fruit of "doing" is that of bringing forth after his kind—Christian work—even another Christian. Every Christian should reproduce himself. The Christian that is slack in his prayer life is deficient in bearing the fruit of "being" and the fruit of "doing." The secret of spiritual power and fruitfulness is tarrying much in the secret closet of prayer. Secret closet praying will bring open rewards.

I. Prayer Spells Spiritual Power

We all remember the spelling lessons in school. When a word was not spelled correctly, the teacher said "wrong." If spelled correctly, the teacher said "right." Prayer is the right way to obtain spiritual power. The person who has the power of the Spirit resting upon him certainly is a person of prayer.

A young man, who had just started out in the ministry, possessed unusual spiritual power. He was inexperienced, and not highly trained; however, he was a mystery unto many. Different people said they could not understand why he possessed so much power and had such great success. Others enquired, "How can a young man possess such great power and an inexplainable influence for good which so greatly moves people?" An aged saintly woman exclaimed that she understood why this young man possessed great spiritual power. Her reply was, "That young man is very thick with the Lord." That is what spelled spiritual power in his life. Prayer will spell power in your life.

II. Prayer Leads to Success

The person who would seek to become a success should faithfully follow the pathway of prayer. The defeated person does not need to go far to discover the reason for his defeats. They come from a lack of prayer. The prayerful person is also a successful person.

A church in the East was teeming with spiritual life and success under the leadership of a faithful, praying pastor. Another minister coveted to learn the secret of his success. He went to visit this church, and found the aged colored caretaker in the church. He spoke to him, saying, "You have a great preacher, haven't you?"

"Yes, Sah. We have the best preacher under God's shinin' sun, Sah."

"What makes him so powerful?" asked the visitor.

"Ah do not know, Sah, but he sho am a powerful man."

"Would you show me through the church?"

"Yes, Sah; be glad to, Sah."

He said, "I would like to see the preacher's study."

"Now," he said, "if it isn't asking too much, would you be kind enough to tell me exactly what your preacher does in the morning before he goes into the pulpit? Does he attend the church school?"

"Yes, Sah. He always attends the church school, Sah."

"What does he do when the church school is over? Let me be your preacher. You tell me what to do."

"Yes, Sah. You go to that desk and sit in that chair. That's what our preacher does every Sunday morning, Sah. Now jes' cry like yo' heart is breakin'."

"But," said the visiting minister, "I can't. I don't feel like it."

"Then," the old colored man said, "I'se afraid yo' can't preach like our preacher preaches, Sah, cause that's what he does, Sah."

Every Christian will find the secret of success in the secret closet of prayer.

III. Prayer Brings Victory

When much time is spent in prayer, and in living in touch with God, a spiritual reserve of power is stored up that will enable us to stand in the day of trial. Prayer will help us to endure in defensive warfare, and also enable us to engage in an offensive spiritual warfare. Victory always comes to the person who is fortified by the walls of prayer.

IV. Prayer Begets Holy Desires

Holy desires are normal to a deeply spiritual person. Holy desires are begotten in the secret place of prayer. Prayer leads to holy desires, and holy desires lead to prayer. One enhances and intensifies the other. The less a person prays, the less he cares for the spiritual, heavenly, and eternal things. The more time that is spent in prayer, the more intense the desires become for God, spirituality, and heaven. All holy desires are begotten by the Holy Spirit in us. He does not beget these desires to tantalize or mock us, but to bring them to fruition in our lives.

V. Prayer Opens Closed Doors

Prayer is nothing less than talking to God. We are limited, but He is omnipotent. Praying is asking God to do that which we are not able to do. He will answer the prayer of faith. The Lord can open doors which no man can shut. The person who prays much will have open doors. Any who do not have open doors should search their prayer life to see if there is a lack along that line. The person who prays much need not fear of continuously closed doors. The Lord will open doors and provide a way. One of the saddest things in the Christian life is that of a person who once prayed much, and was greatly used and blessed by the Lord in Christian work, but now prays little; therefore, the Lord has set him aside, or on a shelf. This is a spiritual tragedy.

The apostle Paul never lacked for an open door. When the Spirit forbade and restrained him from preaching in Asia Minor, it was that He might lead him into a greater and more needy field. It is not stated that Paul prayed; however, it is reasonable to assume he did pray about open doors and where he should go. He taught and wrote that we should "Pray without ceasing," and certainly he practiced what he preached. He lived up-to-date in his prayer life; therefore, it was easy for the Lord to reveal His will to him.

VI. Prayer Digs a Well of Joy

Prayer brings us nigh to God and also brings God nigh to us. Any person may draw nigh to God when he approaches the throne of grace in the spirit of worship and prayer. There is no joy like the joy of meeting God, and the joy which His presence and blessings bring.

"We all may meet in the same sweet place,
When we ardently meet at the throne of grace."

David had experienced the joy of the presence and blessing of the Lord. He wrote from actual experience, "In Thy presence is fulness of joy; at Thy right hand there are pleasures for evermore" (Ps. 16:11).

Fanny Crosby, the sainted blind song-writer experienced the joy of communion with God. She very beautifully expressed the joy of communion with God in prayer in the following words:

"Oh, the pure delight of a single hour
That before Thy throne I spend,
When I kneel in prayer, and with Thee my God,
I commune as friend with friend."

This joy made her heart cry out in a melodious prayer for a closer fellowship, even that of being at the Savior's side.

"Draw me nearer, nearer, nearer, blessed Lord,
To the cross where Thou hast died;
Draw me nearer, nearer, nearer, blessed Lord,
To Thy precious bleeding side.

Prayer will keep the well of joy open and the stream of joy flowing. If the well has become clogged with the cares of life, the deceitfulness of riches, or the material things, it may be re-dug by prayer and confession, and kept open by daily draughts of joy experienced by daily prayer.

VII. Prayer Tenderizes the Spirit

By lingering much in the presence of the Lord, we become more like Him, the object of our worship. In prayer we imbibe His nature, and take on His virtues and qualities. The more we absorb of Christ, the more we become like Him. He possesses the virtues of compassion, kindness, mercy, grace, a forgiving spirit, and a love which led Him to die to save lost souls. Prayer will make the soul very susceptible to the spiritual, holy, and heavenly things. The person who comes short in his prayer life fails to absorb of the spirit of Christ; therefore, he becomes cold and critical. It is then he fails to see his own faults and the virtues in others, but becomes critical; and the best people will seem hypocritical to him. His own spirit has become cold, critical, and self-centered. But the person who prays much becomes tender in spirit, Christlike in nature, and will possess a forgiving spirit; then he will see the good in others.

Have you felt a spiritual lack in your life? Would you like to possess spiritual power? Does your heart long for spiritual success? Do you need more victories? Would you cherish holy desires? Do you want open doors? Are you lacking in joy? Would you appreciate a greater compassion for lost souls, a more tender spirit, and a greater love for Christ? You will find the positive answers to all these questions if you will linger much in the secret closet with the Lord in humility, in confession, and prayer.

CHAPTER VII

POSITIVE REASONS FOR UNANSWERED PRAYER

There are some positive reasons for unanswered prayers, even as there are negative reasons for unanswered prayers. The aggressive Christian will be greatly concerned that his prayers shall be answered. The Bible is the best book on prayer. It should be read and studied with an objective of knowing how to get answers to our prayers. If they are not answered, certainly there are reasons for them not being answered. The Bible will explain why they are not answered. An unconcern about unanswered prayers reveals a lack in the life of a Christian.

I. Priding Self in Personal Righteousness

"There they cry, but none giveth answer, because of the pride of evil men. Surely God will not hear vanity, neither will the Almighty regard it" (Job 35:12, 13).

"The Pharisee stood and prayed thus with himself, God, I thank Thee, that I am not as other men are, extortioners, unjust, adulterers, or even as this publican. I fast twice in the week, I give tithes of all that I possess. And the publican, standing afar off, would not lift up so much as his eyes unto heaven, but smote upon his breast, saying, God be merciful to me a sinner. I tell you, this man went down to his house justified rather than the other: for every one that exalteth himself shall be abased; and he that humbleth himself shall be exalted" (Luke 18:11-14).

The self-righteous Pharisee came to the temple to pray. He did not pray to God, but he "prayed with himself." This Pharisee was exceedingly self-righteous, proud, and boastful. His prayer was a self-indulgence; therefore, vain and mockery. He had no desire for anything, did not ask for anything, and his prayer was not offered as in the presence of God; but he praised himself, boasted of his goodness and works, and condemned the publican. He employed the perpendicular, personal pronoun "I" six times. His prayer was negative; therefore, the Lord did not justify him. Pride in a person's heart or prayers will hinder his prayers from going through. From the publican's prayer we learn that humility, the opposite of pride, is a potent factor in getting our prayers through to God, which assures an answer.

II. Disobeying God's Laws

"He that turneth away his ear from hearing the law, even his prayer shall be abomination" (Prov. 28:9).

We speak to God by prayer. He speaks to us through His Word, His Spirit, divine providences, and through His ministering servants. When we obey Him, He will hearken to us. When we do not obey His laws, His laws will not become obedient to us. When God's laws are disregarded, He will not regard our prayers, but they will be an abomination to Him. God will justly refuse to hear those who do not heed His laws. When our prayers are not answered, we should check up on ourselves to see if any of His laws are being disregarded.

III. Regarding Iniquity in the Heart

"If I regard iniquity in my heart, the Lord will not hear me" (Ps. 66:18).

God hates sin with an infinite hatred. On the other hand He loves righteousness. To be like God we must hate sin and love righteousness. To regard sin means to see, to look at, to look at with favor, to respect, to approve. Since God hates sin and looks at it with an abhorrence, we need to take the same attitude toward sin. When we do not hate what He hates and love what He loves, we are not like Him. If we cherish something He hates, we must get rid of that before He will answer our prayers. When sin gets between us and God, that will rule our prayers out and make them void.

IV. Offering Unworthy Service to God

"Ye offer polluted bread upon Mine altar; and ye say, Wherein have we polluted Thee? In that ye say, The table of the

Lord is contemptible. And if ye offer the blind for sacrifice, is it not evil? and if ye offer the lame and sick, is it not evil? offer it now unto thy governor; will he be pleased with thee, or accept thy person? saith the Lord of hosts. And now, I pray you, beseech God that He will be gracious unto us: this hath been by your means: will He regard your persons? saith the Lord of hosts" (Mal. 1:7-9).

God demands our best, and is worthy of it. In Old Testament times all offerings brought to Him had to be the best, without any spots or blemishes. When they were not the best, He did not accept them. God gave His best to redeem us, and in return He asks our best. In the days of Malachi the people offered the blind, the diseased, and the lame to the Lord. They also offered polluted bread to Him, and would not offer any service without being paid for it. The Lord did not accept their sacrifices for they were an abomination to Him. When any person offers the Lord the scraps, the refuse, the leavings, and the fag ends, or that which he does not want, or after he has indulged in what he wants, such service, offerings, or anything else will not be accepted by the Lord. That person does not deserve God's attention or blessings. When our sacrifice and service to Him are no cost to us, they will not move Him to hearken to us. The widow who gave two mites greatly moved the Lord. Should a millionaire offer two thousand dollars to the Lord when he owed Him one hundred thousand dollars in tithes, that would not move the Lord, for the Lord would consider what he had left. Those who do not offer God their best need not expect answers to their prayers. The way to get our prayers answered is to offer God our best, even a sacrifice and a service which are pure and unblemished, then God will hearken to our prayers.

V. Asking Amiss

"Ye ask, and receive not, because ye ask amiss" (James 4:3).

Asking amiss is another positive reason for unanswered prayer. Asking amiss may include a number of things, such as asking perversely, for our own pleasures, for selfish motives, for those things which

God does not want us to have, or for those things which are not good for us. God wisely considers our petitions; and when they are not for His glory, or our good, He will not give us what we have asked.

VI. Praying with a Selfish Motive

"Ye ask, and receive not, because ye ask amiss, that ye may consume it upon your lusts" (James 4:3).

Lust is an unlawful love and an overdesire, a sinful desire. If people could receive from God the gratification of lustful desires, there is no doubt they would pray to become millionaires, famous, beautiful, popular, to live long without becoming aged, to escape death, to excell others, to become highly gifted, to become champions, and many other things. These things might become detrimental to them and detract from God's glory. When anything is asked in prayer to be consumed on our own lust, that prayer will not be answered.

VII. Wavering at God's Promises

"But let him ask in faith, nothing wavering. For he that wavereth is like a wave of the sea driven with the wind and tossed. For let not that man think that he shall receive any thing of the Lord" (James 1:6, 7).

The person who is steady and faithful will be honored by God in his prayer life. God's promises are conditioned on faith and obedience. The person who allows doubts to control him and disobeys will be beset with unbelief. Doubts are like the wind and waves on a sea. Wavering in faith is like a ship tossed by the wind and waves. To live a life of faith is to be lifted up, and to doubt is to be cast down. The person who fluctuates, that is, mounts up toward heaven and lives in the glories intent on entering heaven, desiring to secure immortality, expressing a determination to be faithful to the Lord even unto death, then sinks into doubt and despair, seeking the ease of the body, worldly enjoyments, and pleasures, is likened to the waves of the sea which rise and fall. Such a life is far from being satisfactory to self and to the Lord. It will hinder faith and the prayer life. An eye that is single to the glory of

God, a heart that is fixed, a mind that has a single interest in the heavenly, spiritual, and eternal things, and a face set like a flint, will be honored by God and move Him to answer prayer.

CHAPTER VIII

NEGATIVE CAUSES FOR UNANSWERED PRAYER

The electrician must obey the laws of electricity before the laws of electricity become obedient to him. Even so, the Christian must obey the laws of true prayer before the laws of prayer become responsive to him. It is essential for us to obey what God has commanded in His Word before He will give us what He has promised in His Word. Some prayers are not answered because of negative reasons, that is, the right laws of prayer have not been met. Often it may be just a very small thing out of place which prevents a machine from running, or the electrical current from passing through the wires. A little interference may hinder the prayer communication from going through. When the right conditions are met, God will answer prayer.

I. Because We Do Not Have Any Prayers to be Answered

"Ye have not, because ye ask not" (James 4:2).

When we consider the many prayer promises which God has given us in His Word, the many inducements we have to urge us to pray, the willingness of God to answer prayer, the great need for prayer, and the great accomplishments wrought through prayer, the great wonder and mystery is that people pray so little. James made a very simple, yet positive, statement that needs little comment when he wrote, "Ye have not, because ye ask not." This is exactly the state of some people, they do not ask. Here is one of the negative "causes" for no answers to prayer. They do not have any prayers to be answered.

II. Because Our Prayers are Not Properly Addressed

"When ye pray, say, Our Father which art in heaven" (Luke 11:2).

Our prayers are to be addressed to the Father or to Christ. Many prayers are prayed at other people, not to God. Others are offered to be heard only by people and to make a good impression on them. Again, many prayers are said with no conscious knowledge of God, with no reverence to His name. Then prayer may be offered to deceive other people, or to cover things in the sight of men. These prayers are not addressed to God's office. Let us remember, when we pray and address our prayers to God's office, that His office is not in our neighbor's care. Prayers that are offered from the head, which are pompous, merely vociferous, eloquent, or cold, and not from the heart, also are illegible; therefore, get lost on the way. These are some "causes" of prayers being unanswered. It is claimed that over two million letters go to the dead letter office in the United States every year because they are not properly addressed. Many prayers never reach the throne of grace because they are not properly addressed.

III. Because the Cry of the Poor is Not Heeded

"Whoso stoppeth his ears at the cry of the poor, he also shall cry himself, but shall not be heard" (Prov. 21:13).

There is a universal law that whatsoever a man soweth, that shall he also reap. We once as sinners were poor and cried unto the Lord. He heard our cry in our spiritual poverty and answered our prayer. When others are in need and cry to us for help and we close our ears to their cry, when we cry to the Lord He will not hear us. The Lord will treat us even as we treat others. God will be deaf to the prayers of those who are deaf to the cries of the poor.

IV. Because We Do Not Possess a Forgiving Spirit

"And when ye stand praying, forgive, if ye have ought against any: that your Father also which is in heaven may forgive you your trespasses. But if ye do not forgive, neither will your Father which is in heaven forgive your trespasses" (Mark 11:25, 26).

The elements of an unforgiving spirit include an envious spirit, a jealous spirit, not taking delight in the triumph and success of others, or too stern a spirit in disciplining others. Where these things exist, they will hinder prayers from being answered. The very opposite attitude needs to be taken, even that of preferring others to ourselves, delighting in others who excel us, and in pushing others to the front. Doing these things will be a great means of getting our prayers through. The Lord has forgiven the Christian many sins which were a debt he never could pay; therefore, he should hold a forgiving and compassionate spirit toward everybody. This will be remembered by the Lord when he prays.

V. Because We Do Not Hearken to God's Voice

"Therefore it is come to pass, that as He cried, and they would not hear; so they cried, and I would not hear, saith the Lord of hosts" (Zech. 7:13).

In the days of Zechariah, the prophet, the Jews were guilty of not heeding the cry of the Lord to them in time of prosperity when they were given to iniquity. The time came when they cried to Him in the day of their trouble that the Lord would remove His judgments and wrath from them, but He would not hear them. When we heed His voice, He will respond to our voice. When we obey Him, He will obey us; and when we say yes to Him, He will say yes to us. On the other hand, those who take an obstinate and negative attitude

toward God will meet the same from Him, and discover their prayer answers will be negative instead of
positive.

VI. Because Prayers Are Not Offered with a True Motive

"And when thou prayest, thou shalt not be as the hypocrites
are: for they love to pray standing in the synagogues and in the
corners of the streets, that they may be seen of men. Verily I
say unto you, They have their reward" (Matt. 6:5).

The Pharisees prayed to attract the attention of
men and not the attention of God. They were more concerned about what men thought of their prayers than
what God thought. Their prayers were offered specifically for men to hear and not God. The praise of men was
sought rather than the favor of God. God was not
honored or pleased with their prayers. A selfish motive
activated their prayers. No faith accompanied their
prayers, neither did they expect an answer. God was
not moved by their praying. All they sought was the
praise of men, and when they obtained that, they were
satisfied. Such prayers were not offered with a true
motive. This rendered them negative and grounded
them; and, of course, they were not answered.

VII. Because Husbands and Wives Do Not Render Due Regard to Each Other

"Likewise, ye wives, be in subjection to your own husbands;
that, if any obey not the word, they also may without the word
be won by the conversation of the wives; while they behold your
chaste conversation coupled with fear. Whose adorning let it not
be that outward adorning of plaiting the hair, and of wearing of
gold, or of putting on of apparel; but let it be the hidden man of
the heart, in that which is not corruptible, even the ornament of
a meek and quiet spirit, which is in the sight of God of great
price. For after this manner in the old time the holy women
also, who trusted in God, adorned themselves, being in subjection
unto their own husbands: Even as Sara obeyed Abraham, calling him lord: whose daughters ye are, as long as ye do well, and
are not afraid with any amazement. Likewise, ye husbands,
dwell with them according to knowledge, giving honor unto the
wife, as unto the weaker vessel, and as being heirs together of

the grace of life; that your prayers be not hindered" (I Peter 3:1-7).

The above Scripture verses teach much. They teach how a Christian wife may win to the Lord a sinner husband who does not go to church. First, she must live in subjection to her husband and recognize him as head over her. There is nothing derogatory in a wife being in subjection to her husband. When she honors, reverences, and promotes him, she being one with him, he will lift her up; and she will share that promotion. The Christian wife may win her sinner husband to the Lord by her "conversation." "Conversation," here means the entire tenor of her life, that is, her words, actions, cheerfulness, interest, submission, chastity, etc., in relation to him. She needs to put on exhibition before him that he may "behold her chaste conversation coupled with fear," which is a loving, cheerful, respectful fear. Her adorning should not be that of a worldly spirit, nor for a carnal purpose, nor for vain show, but rather of a modest and retiring (keeping self hidden) manner, and let "the hidden man of the heart" be adorned. This is done by manifesting the Christian virtues and graces, and by possessing "a meek and quiet spirit" (disposition). A wife's most powerful weapons for handling her husband are her cheerfulness and silence. These are of great price in the sight of the Lord. When she does as she is admonished by the Lord, the Lord will help her in her prayer life, and also to save her husband. The husband—presumably a Christian husband—also is admonished. His part is to dwell with his wife according to knowledge, that is, the Scriptures; to manifest those qualities which he knows tend toward love and peace; to honor his wife by praising her; to do the hard work and provide for her comforts; and to acknowledge that she is on an equality in the Lord and an heir of salvation. When they are united as a compound unity, a mutual relation exists in all things; and, when there is a oneness of heart, desires, and mind, that relationship will be pleasing to the Lord. Living like this Scripture admonishes is in a wife's favor in obtaining answers to her prayers, and unitedly they will be able to greatly move God by their prayers. When a wife, a husband, or a couple, do not obey this inspired admonition, they may know the "cause" of unanswered prayers.

CHAPTER IX

SECRET CLOSET PRAYING

Christ gave us one of the greatest lessons on prayer when He said, "But thou, when thou prayest, enter in-to thy closet, and when thou hast shut thy door, pray to thy Father which is in secret; and thy Father which seeth in secret shall reward thee openly" (Matt. 6:6). The secret for open rewards is prayer in the secret closet. The Christian who fails to pray in secret will come far short in the Christian life in public. Many great problems must be prayed through and settled when alone with God in prayer. One devout Christian said that when he went one day without spending much time in secret prayer, he keenly felt it; if two days, other Christians discerned it; and if three days, the world or sinners recognized it. The Christian may offer silent prayers in company, which is to be classed as private prayer. This should be freely practiced, but it does not take the place of secret closet prayer.

I. Jacob was Alone with God all Night

"And Jacob was left alone; and there wrestled a man with him until the breaking of the day" (Gen. 32:24).

The thing which was the means of Jacob coming to the front and becoming great was the two nights in which he was alone. The first one was at Bethel. This was the night in which the God of Abraham and of Isaac became the God of Jacob. A crisis experience took place in his life that night. This was the first night in which he was alone and away from home as far as we have any record. This was when he fled from his angry brother Esau to go to Padan-aram to seek a wife. Up to this time Jacob depended on his mother's religion and his father's God. That night in the open field, with stones for his pillows, God met him and talked to him, and Jacob talked to the Lord. This prepared him to leave his country, and for the journey. Then he went on his way rejoicing. The best thing that could have happened to Jacob was to be alone with God one night. This certainly was the night of his conversion. Twenty years later when he returned, another crisis came in his life in which it was necessary for him to be alone again. We read, "And Jacob was left alone." This again was the best thing that could have happened to him. The Lord met him, wrestled with him, subdued him, touched his thigh and put it out of joint, and changed his inward nature. Jacob arose a cripple, but a prince of God, who now had power with God and man. This prepared him to enter the land and to meet his angry brother and an army of four hundred armed men. There was an unseen influence and a mightily felt power that overpowered Esau and his band, which brought them together in submission and reconciliation. Without this experience Jacob would not have been qualified to meet his angry brother. The results would have been disastrous. As a result of being alone God prevailed in his life; then Jacob was qualified to prevail with God, which he did, and that is why he prevailed with four hundred and one armed men.

II. Elijah was Alone with God Much of His Life

"And the word of the Lord came unto him, saying, Get thee hence, and turn thee eastward, and hide thyself by the brook Cherith, that is before Jordan" (I Kings 17:2, 3).

Elijah's first appearance was before king Ahab. He gave this idolatrous king a short but startling message that there would not be dew or rain these years according to his word. Then he fled for his life, and the Lord told him where to hide. He prayed, James says, and it rained not for the space of three years and six months. It was while he was alone that he was given to prayer. This gave him time to pray. Being alone prepared him to appear before the king, before the Baal worshipers, and before an idolatrous nation. God was with him in public because he was much with the Lord

in secret. This will be true with any person. Those
who would have the Lord with them in public and
achieve great victories before men must seclude themselves; then, alone with God in prayer, fight the battle,
obtain the victory, the anointing, the courage, and the
fortitude in secret which will assure victory and an
open reward in public.

III. Daniel Prayed Much While Alone with God

"In those days I Daniel was mourning three full weeks.
Therefore I was left alone, and saw this great vision, and there
remained no strength in me: for my comeliness was turned in
me into corruption, and I retained no strength" (Dan. 10:2, 8).

"Now when Daniel knew that the writing was signed, he
went into his house; and his windows being open in his chamber
toward Jerusalem, he kneeled upon his knees three times a day,
and prayed, and gave thanks before his God, as he did aforetime"
(Dan. 6:10).

Daniel was a man of prayer. He was a choice character and a great saint. Greatly beloved and greatly
hated was he. Daniel was greatly beloved by God and
angels, and greatly hated by Satan and wicked men.
It seemed that heaven took a great interest in him and
made much over him. Everything seemed to work
against him, but, like Joseph, he came out on top. From
the entire tenor of his life, we are led to assume that
he prayed much. He was a man of holy desires, courage,
trials, visions, principles, and prayer. He prayed as a
young man in Jerusalem, having been influenced by
the prophet Jeremiah and the good king Josiah. He
prayed about his lessons, his food, the concern of Nebuchadnezzar's dream, before he was cast into the lions'
den, concerning the prophetic visions he received, concerning the release of the Jews from captivity, and for
Babylon in which he lived. The fact that he prayed
much in secret explains why he received so many open
rewards.

IV. John the Baptist was Alone Until the Day of His Appearance

"And the child grew, and waxed strong in spirit, and was in
the deserts till the day of his shewing unto Israel" (Luke 1:80).

John the Baptist was a unique character. His life was spent in solitude. He was alone much of the time, and lived in seclusion. It also is inferred that he was a man of great prayer and a teacher of prayer (Luke 11:1). He taught his followers just what he practiced. Being alone much gave him time to pray, to meditate, and for his call to burn in his heart so that when he made his public appearance, he had a burning message, which he delivered in the power and inspiration of the Spirit.

V. Christ was Alone all Night in Prayer

"And when He had sent the multitude away, He went up into a mountain apart to pray: and when the evening was come, He was there alone" (Matt. 14:23).

As a Man Christ knew the value of prayer. It was a great delight to Him to get alone and commune with His Father. He spent forty days in the wilderness alone being tempted by Satan. The result of being alone was He returned in the power of the Spirit and began to make social contacts. On several different occasions we read that Christ sought retirement that He might pray. Retirement to be alone with God for prayer and meditation is very essential. This we learn from the example of Christ and of all great spiritual men. Social contacts are essential, however, religious retirement needs to come first in order to make the social contacts effective. One without the other is not complete. It is not God's thought that the Christian shall practice spiritual isolationism. Christ did not do so, nor should Christians do so. Neither should the Christian practice continual social contacts. The spiritual retirement is essential for the Christian to receive his spiritual recuperation, and the social contact is needful for the sinner, that he may become awakened and quickened by the Spirit through the testimony of the Christian.

VI. Paul Spent Much Time Alone in Prayer

"We give thanks to God and the Father of our Lord Jesus Christ, praying always for you" (Col. 1:3).

Paul was a man given to prayer. From the book of Acts and the Epistles which he wrote, we learn that he prayed much. In his writings he has much to say about prayer. The secret of his power and success was that he prayed much in secret. Little may we realize how much time great saints spend in private prayer. That is not for us to know, but it is a secret between the saint and God. The open reward is certain. The years Paul spent in prison gave him more time to pray. This bore fruit in the production of his richest and deepest writings, The Prison Epistles.

VII. Your Possibilities When Alone in Prayer with God

"The effectual fervent prayer of a righteous man availeth much" (James 5:16b).

That which has been true in the lives of many saints, that is, power, victory and success crowned their ministry as a result of much private prayer, may become true in your life through much time spent in secret closet praying. As the enemies of Christ took knowledge that the apostles had been with Jesus, so the sinners whom you contact will take knowledge that you have been in contact with the Lord, if you spend much time in secret prayer. A great saint one time expressed his great regret that he had spent so little time with God in secret prayer and so much time with men and material things. This is true of most Christian people, that is, they spend too little time in communion with God and too much time with material things. It is hard for the deeply spiritual person to understand any Christian, or minister, who never cares or seeks to be alone. Those who never are alone with God in prayer never accomplish much for the Lord.

CHAPTER X

CONDITIONS ON WHICH GOD ANSWERS PRAYER

There are some people who wonder why their prayers are not answered. We can not do as we please and obtain what we want. If we want what God has promised in His Word, we must do as He commanded in His Word. Let us ever bear in heart and mind that in order for God to answer prayer, we must do our part. The Lord will keep His Word at any cost. He will do as He has promised. Some people deal with the Lord as though they had done their part, had met every condition for their prayers to be answered, but that the Lord must be made willing, or be persuaded to grant their request. It seems they want to do God's part, make Him willing, overpersuade Him, make Him see their viewpoint, then He will give them what they want. This is not true prayer. All who want answers to their prayers should become concerned about doing their full duty to God, and of meeting the conditions He has prescribed in His Word. Let us study what the conditions are which God has prescribed in His Word, then cheerfully meet them.

I. Seeking God with All the Heart

"Then shall ye call upon Me, and ye shall go and pray unto Me, and I will hearken unto you. And ye shall seek Me, and find Me, when ye shall search for Me with all your heart. And I will be found of you, saith the Lord" (Jer. 29:12-14).

Observe man's "shalls" and God's "wills." Man's "shalls" come before God's "wills." Man's part is to call, pray, seek, and search after God with all the heart. This can not be done halfheartedly and release God's will. It must be "with all the heart." Ask yourself the question, Have I been truly calling upon God? Have I been really praying? Have I been seeking Him as if I had lost a great fortune? Have I searched for Him with all my heart? The Lord knows. He searches our hearts, weighs our thoughts, and analyzes our motives. He knows when we have met these conditions, and when they are met, His "wills" will be released, and He will do as He has promised.

II. Waiting on the Lord

"I waited patiently for the Lord; and He inclined unto me, and heard my cry" (Psalm 40:1).

"But they that wait upon the Lord shall renew their strength; they shall mount up with wings as eagles; they shall run, and not be weary; and they shall walk, and not faint" (Isa. 40:31).

Waiting on the Lord is a condition men must meet if they want to obtain answers to prayer. Much is included and implied in this word "wait." It eliminates and excludes the "hurry-up" spirit. The spirit of most people is to hurry, hurry, hurry. They hurry through their meals, hurry to work, hurry home, hurry all day long; and if they pray at all (maybe only when dire circumstances force them to it), they hurry to the place of prayer, and hurry through their prayers, and hurry God in answering them, but get nothing, and wonder why God has not answered their prayers. This is not true praying; neither is God obligated to answer their prayers, for they absolutely have not met the condition.

To wait on the Lord means to take time to be holy, to be calm in the soul, and to give God time to answer in His own time and way. Again, to really wait on the Lord implies that we have met every condition and have done all our part. A person cannot really wait for a train, expecting to go somewhere, until he is all ready to go, has dressed, "packed up," purchased his ticket and checked his baggage. Then and only then can he wait for the train.

Then the word "wait" implies service, of serving the Lord, doing as He bids, then coming back for more orders. Such a person will obtain the "tips" from the

Lord which will cause him to be renewed, to mount up, to fly, to run, to walk and not faint.

III. Asking in Faith

"All things, whatsoever ye shall ask in prayer, believing, ye shall receive" (Matt. 21:22).

The one time and all time condition for receiving answers to our prayers is faith. Obedience to God will aid and inspire faith in God. Faith and obedience are inseparable. Faith in God will not operate when there is disobedience to God. Where obedience is cheerfully rendered to the Lord, faith operates automatically and spontaneously. Faith is not exercised by straining the intellect or muscles, but is a restful hope, trust, and repose in God.

IV. Asking According to God's Will

"And this is the confidence that we have in Him, that, if we ask any thing according to His will, He heareth us" (I John 5:14).

If we want what God has for us, we can have what we want. Too many people want only what they want, but do not want what the Lord wants them to have; then they wonder why the Lord does not answer their prayers. God will not answer the prayers of those who have selfish motives or live selfishly. Let us find out what the Lord wants us to have. This we may do by reading His Word and observing His promises. Doing this will help our faith, for He will do as He has promised in His Word; and what He has promised, we do well to believe, for that honors Him.

V. Setting Our Love on God

"Because he hath set his love upon Me, therefore will I deliver him: I will set him on high, because he hath known My name. He shall call upon Me, and I will answer him: I will be with him in trouble; I will deliver him, and honor him" (Psalm 91:14, 15).

This is a great and gracious promise. We receive much for little. Our part is to set our love upon Him, to know His name, and to call upon Him. He has commanded that we love Him with all our heart, soul, strength, and mind. This takes in all there is of us, and

involves a good Christian experience. To know His
name means to truly know Him and to possess His
nature; and to call on Him is true prayer. His promise
is to give us deliverance, edification, answer our prayer,
give us His constant presence and promotion.

VI. Abiding in Christ

"If ye abide in Me, and My words abide in you, ye shall ask
what ye will, and it shall be done unto you" (John 15:7).

Abiding in Christ means to dwell in Him. The word
abide means to dwell, be present, remain, endure,
stand, tarry, and to continue. This means that we have
a holy heart, are firm and faithful in the Christian life.
By His Word abiding in us means that we are doing as
He has commanded us and that which is agreeable to
His Word. When we live by His Word, according to His
Word, and His Word is abiding in us, the promise will
come true in our lives. This is true union with Christ,
and leads to communion with God and disunion with
the world. Abiding in Christ means we are in Him as
the branch is in the vine. We draw our strength from
Him. The heavenly Father is the Husbandman and
exercises every care over the Vine (Christ) and the
branches (believers), and is glorified in answering our
prayers.

VII. Keeping God's Commandments

"And whatsoever we ask, we receive of Him, because we
keep His commandments, and do those things that are pleasing
in His sight" (I John 3:22).

There are two conditions in this Scripture which
the Christian is to meet, namely, the keeping of His
commandments and the doing of those things which
are pleasing in His sight. The keeping of His commandments is more than doing them by a motive im-
posed by compulsion. It is keeping them with a
jealous care and from a motive of delight. It is obeying them from the standpoint of "want to" instead of
a "have to."

Doing those things which are pleasing in His sight
is going farther yet. A son who has disobeyed his

father by failing to do as he commanded him can not come to him and ask for anything in faith, for down in his heart he does not expect it, and he well knows he does not deserve it. The son who cheerfully has finished the task his father gave to him and has done much more has not only kept his commandments but has also done those things which are pleasing in his sight. He can come to his father and ask in faith and courage, and really receive what he asks. So with the Christian, when he has kept God's commandments and gone farther, even done that which is pleasing in His sight, will receive what he asks.

CHAPTER XI

PRAYERS OF ONE DESIRE

It is not always the prayer that asks for the most things, or that covers the longest period of time, or that prays clear around the world, or that prays for everybody in general, that amounts to the most, or obtains the greatest answer; but rather, it is the prayer that is specific, earnest, and of one supreme desire that moves God and gets what it has asked. It is better to ask for one thing with an earnest desire and receive it than to ask for many things with no concern whether any will be received or not. God is pleased when we are positive in our asking. We should pray for the need of the hour. Bring your needs to Him and ask for that which you really need, or that which He wants to give, then expect a definite objective answer. To do so, there needs to be a sincere heart desire in order to be positive, pointed, earnest, believing, and fervent in our praying. Seven Bible examples are selected to show that the prayer of one earnest desire brought to each a specific answer.

I. Abraham's Prayer for Lot's Deliverance

"And Abraham drew near, and said, Wilt Thou also destroy the righteous with the wicked? Peradventure there be fifty righteous within the city . . . forty and five . . . and forty . . . thirty . . . twenty . . . ten . . . and He said, I will not destroy it for ten's sake" (Gen. 18:23-32).

When the Lord revealed to Abraham that He was about to destroy Sodom, he became definitely concerned about Lot and his family. Abraham asked six petitions, each one bearing specifically on the one objective of Lot's deliverance, and each succeeding petition became more specific than the preceding one. The Lord answered each petition in the affirmative. Though there were not ten righteous persons in Sodom, the Lord answered Abraham's prayer. Two angels went to Sodom and delivered Lot. As they brought him forth, one said, "Haste thee, escape thither; for I cannot do anything till thou be come thither." It was the intercession of Abraham that prevented disaster from taking place before Lot was out of the danger zone. During the process of the destruction of the cities of the plain, it is stated that "God remembered Abraham, and sent Lot out of the midst of the overthrow, when He overthrew the cities in the which Lot dwelt."

II. Eliezer's Prayer for a Bride for Isaac

"And he said, O Lord God of my master Abraham . . . send me good speed this day . . . let it come to pass . . . let the same be she that Thou hast appointed . . . and it came to pass" (Gen. 24:12-15).

Eliezer, Abraham's servant, was very specific in the prayer he offered to the God of Abraham. He had one great desire, and that was that he might not make a mistake, but that he might select the right damsel which should become the bride for Isaac. He stipulated the conditions unto the Lord and the proposition he would propose to the damsel for a basis on which he would proceed in securing her. His prayer was very definite and along just one line. God answered his prayer. The damsel was on her way to the well. He made his request, and then she proceeded to do exactly as stipulated in the proposition which he had made to the Lord. He acknowledged his answer to the Lord and worshiped Him. He proceeded on that basis and secured her, because God was in it and answered his prayer.

III. Moses' Prayer for Miriam's Healing

"And Moses cried unto the Lord, saying, Heal her now, O God, I beseech Thee" (Num. 12:13).

Miriam and Aaron spoke against Moses. They became jealous of him, which was sin on their part. The Lord swiftly visited judgment on Miriam and she became leprous all over. Leprosy did not break out in

Aaron, for he was God's high priest; however, he admitted his sin and folly, and said, "Alas, my lord, I beseech thee, lay not the sin upon us, wherein we have done foolishly, and wherein we have sinned." Moses, in his meekness and patience graciously and instantly prayed to the Lord an earnest, yet short, and positive prayer for Miriam's healing. The Lord healed Miriam instantly, but as a punishment for her folly she was shut out of the camp for seven days, during which time Israel did not march.

IV. Samson's Prayer for Supernatural Strength

"And Samson called unto the Lord, and said, O Lord God, remember me, I pray Thee, and strengthen me, I pray Thee, only this once, O God, that I may be at once avenged of the Philistines for my two eyes" (Judges 16:28).

This was Samson's final prayer, his dying prayer; and his desire for the answer was so intense it was stronger than the desire for life. This prayer too was very definite, and a prayer of one desire. It was not a general prayer, for general things and the desire for a general answer. The prayer was specific; the request was specific; the desire was specific; the objective was specific; and the answer was specific, which brought specific results.

V. Hannah's Prayer for a Son

"For this child I prayed: and the Lord hath given me my petition which I asked of Him" (I Sam. 1:27).

Hannah was greatly burdened because of the failure of the high priest and his sons, because all the men of Israel were of such quality that God was not able to select a leader, because Israel lived on a low spiritual plane, and because she was childless, which made her an object of reproach. There was begotten one supreme desire in her heart for a son whom she could dedicate to the Lord to become a leader, to lead Israel back to God and bring about a spiritual reformation. For this one thing she prayed, for it was the one supreme desire, ambition, and plan of her life. It expressed itself in a prayer of one petition. The Lord answered her

prayer, gave her a son; and he became a great judge,
prophet, reformer, and revivalist.

VI. Elijah's Prayer for Fire to Fall

"Elijah the prophet came near, and said, Lord God of Abraham, Isaac, and of Israel, let it be known this day that Thou art
God in Israel, and that I am Thy servant, and that I have done
all these things at Thy word. Hear me, O Lord, hear me, that
this people may know that Thou art the Lord God, and that Thou
hast turned their heart back again. Then the fire of the Lord
fell, and consumed the burnt sacrifice" (I Kings 18:36-38).

Elijah on Mt. Carmel was greatly concerned about
one thing, and that was that fire might fall on his sacrifice in order that all Israel might know that the Lord
God was the true God and Baal was only a dumb idol.
His prayer consisted of only sixty-three words. This
was not a long prayer, but a fervent, specific prayer,
which would require less than forty seconds to offer
intelligently. God answered this prayer instantly, and
the fire fell. The people saw it fall, and observed that
it consumed the sacrifice, the stones, and the water.
They all acknowledged, "The Lord, He is the God; the
Lord, He is the God."

VII. Blind Man's Prayer for Sight

"And he cried, saying, Jesus, Thou Son of David, have mercy
on me . . . And he said, Lord, that I may receive my sight" (Luke
18:38, 41).

Blind Bartimaeus had one desire and offered a
prayer of one petition, that was for his sight. His prayer
was a cry, and his cry was a prayer. When Christ called
him, he threw away his garment. He did not want one
thing to hinder him in going to Christ. When he had
come to Christ, He asked him, "What wilt thou that I
shall do unto thee?" His petition again was direct and
decisive, even, "Lord, that I may receive my sight." It
was his faith which saved him. Jesus of Nazareth passed
by. It was an hour of crisis. He recognized it; yet he
encountered hindrances, obstructions, discouragements,
and unsympathetic people. He would not be silenced
by the people. The more they suppressed him, the more
insistent he became. He pressed his claim, and obtained

the one thing he desired, even sight. He was richly rewarded. Let us make our prayers decisive and earnest, for this will aid our faith, which moves God to give us the desire of our heart.

CHAPTER XII

TWO POTENT PRAYER FACTORS

"And whatsoever we ask, we receive of Him, because we keep His commandments, and do those things that are pleasing in His sight" (I John 3:22).

A factor is an element that contributes to the production of results. This text reveals two potent factors which are essential in obtaining answers to our prayers. It reveals the "because" and the "and" of answered prayer. These should be understood by every Christian so that he may know what conditions need to be met to obtain the answers to his prayers.

I. Keeping God's Commandments

God's commandments are just and holy, and in the keeping of them there is great reward. His commandments are not grievous. Let us consider four points under the heading of "Keeping His Commandments" in order that we may learn the meaning of keeping them.

1. Studying His Word to Know His Commandments

We are commanded to study the Scriptures that we may be able to show ourselves approved unto God. Then again, we should study the Scriptures that we may know what God desires and requires, to seek light, and not shun it. Not only should we study to know what His commandments are, but that we may know what they mean, so that we may keep them more intelligently.

2. Heeding His Commandments

Heeding means to regard with care, to give special attention to, even to esteem them highly because they are His commandments. There needs to be a disposition on our part to obey them. We honor Him in heeding, that is, in giving special attention to His commandments. They should be kept with a jealous care, even as a woman would keep her diamonds, or a man his wealth. Many place their valuables in a safety deposit box, or in a safe. The Christian should have Christ's commandments securely locked within his heart, and guard them more than he would material wealth.

3. Courting His Commandments

To court His commandments is to fall in love with them, look at them with delight, be attracted by them, run after them and lay hold on them, then embrace them. Then we should tell the Giver how much we love Him and His commandments, and say unto Him as did David when he spoke directly to the Lord, "More to be desired are they than gold, yea, than much fine gold: sweeter also than honey and the honeycomb," and "O how love I Thy law; it is my meditation all the day."

4. Obeying His Commandments

This will be for God's glory and our good. They should be obeyed joyfully because we sincerely delight in them, and not because we feel we have to obey them. Children obey at times because they want to and at other times because they feel they have to. Our obedience should be joyful, explicit, unquestioning, and prompt.

II. Doing Things Pleasing in His Sight

The first half of the text deals with that which we need to do, and the second part with that which we delight to do. This is like going the second mile of the way. God has a heart, a loving heart, and it may be grieved, or it may be made glad. One of the greatest pleasures in life is not the pleasure that is subjective, or what is done to us, but that of bringing joy to others. There is a pleasure that is greater yet, even that of bringing pleasure to the loving heart of God.

1. Delighting in His Commandments

Doing this is not from a motive of fear, but of love.

This is beautifully expressed in the first Psalm where it says, "But his delight is in the law of the Lord; and in His law doth he meditate day and night." By implication meditation means to ruminate, to bring up the cud, then to chew the same. We learn a great lesson from the animals which ruminate. Cattle get great delight in eating grass; then while lying in the shade, regurgitate the grass eaten, then slowly chew the cud, which gives them pleasure, even that of eating continually. When the Christian reads God's laws, and as it were eats them, then meditates therein, or ruminates, which is to bring to mind again and again, he will obtain great pleasure from God's laws, and God will also take a delight in him and answer his prayers.

2. Jealously Guarding His Commandments

Another thing that is pleasing in His sight is to jealously guard His commandments. This means to be grieved if we break them in any little detail, and to be grieved at heart when we see any one else break any of them. Such an attitude will move God to answer our prayers.

3. Going the Second Mile

We go one mile because the law demands it, and then we go the second mile because the law of love constrains us. The Romans had a law, which was in vogue in the days of Christ, that if a Roman soldier came along he could demand any Jew to assist him in carrying his outfit a mile. In obeying this law there was an outside compelling force, but to go the second mile required an inward impelling love. Christ gave this rule to His followers, and when it is observed it pleases Him and gives Him a delight to answer our prayers.

4. Practicing Self-denial

Self-denial, to be genuine, must be voluntary and not compulsory. To deny self is to give up good things, legitimate things, or things which we could keep, or do, and get to heaven. But we deny self that others may be helped to get to heaven. Doing as He commands and doing that which is pleasing in His sight are illustrated in the following illustration:

A father had two sons. He had some business which demanded his attention. Before he left home, he called his sons to him and appointed the work he wanted them to do that day. He had a large patch of potatoes, and commanded each boy to clean the weeds out of ten rows, then if they had any time left they could spend it in play. One son reasoned that it would not take him long to do the work; therefore, he played first with a neighbor boy. The noon hour arrived, and he had not started his task. After dinner he played a while longer; then toward evening he surmised that his father would return soon, and hurried to his work. His father arrived in the evening and found him in the patch cutting weeds, but he was able to clean only five rows by the time the supper call was given. He completed only half of his assignment. The father was happily surprised that the other son had cut the weeds out of twenty rows, or again as many as he was commanded. This son had gone to work promptly and cheerfully. In doing so he cleaned ten rows; and by cutting the weeds out of ten rows he had kept his father's commandment. With much time left to play, he reasoned, "Now I have obeyed my father's commandment; I will not only obey him, but I will also please him;" therefore, he stayed with the task and finished ten more rows. Of course his father was satisfied with his obedience, and well pleased with the pleasure his son took in him. At the supper table one son shunned his father and did not take pleasure in him. He did not feel comfortable in his presence, nor could he look up into his face with pleasure. He had not obeyed his father, but had his own way. The other son felt pleased and delighted in his father's presence. Both boys had been desiring pocket knives. They had seen some in a show window which pleased them well. The price for each knife was fifty cents. After supper the father took an easy chair in the living room, and the obedient son came into his presence with joy and confidence. His father looked up and enquired what was on his mind. The son took his liberty and came to his lap, and said he would like to have one of the fifty cent pocket knives. His father said, "You have been an obedient boy. I will gladly grant you your request. You have obeyed me by cleaning ten rows of potatoes, and also pleased me in cleaning ten more." This son received just what he asked. He left his father and showed his fifty cent piece to his brother, who also desired a knife. The other son entered into the presence of his father; but he possessed no pleasure, no courage, and of course had no faith to receive what he desired. He had not obeyed his father. He hummed and hawed, then cleared his throat. His father enquired what he wanted. He said, "Fa—fa—f-a-t-h-e-r, I would like to have a knife." His father asked him what he did all that day, and why he had not cleaned the weeds out of ten rows of potatoes. He confessed he played with the neighbor boy. His father said, "No, you have not obeyed me, and you do not deserve a pocket knife." He did not receive the answer to his request. So it is with the Christian and the Lord. God answers the prayers of the person who obeys His commandments and does those things which are pleasing in His sight. These are the two potent factors in obtaining answers to prayer.

CHAPTER XIII

LEVERS FOR OUR PRAYERS

God's promises and commandments go hand in hand and run parallel. If we want that which God has promised in His Word, we must do as He has command- ed in His Word. There is no variableness nor shadow of turning with God. Neither can He change that which He has promised. When the conditions of His promises are met, He will keep His Word. The thing for every Christian to do is to find out what the conditions are which act as levers to move God. A lever is a bar used to pry or dislodge something firmly fixed. With a bar a person may pry up something many times heavier than he could lift with his bare hands. Every Christian worker should learn those secrets in the Word of God which will intensify and multiply his praying capacity and accomplishments.

I. Tithing All Our Income

"Bring ye all the tithes into the storehouse, that there may be meat in Mine house, and prove Me now herewith, saith the Lord of hosts, if I will not open you the windows of heaven, and pour you out a blessing, that there shall not be room enough to receive it. And I will rebuke the devourer for your sakes, and he shall not destroy the fruits of your ground; neither shall your vine cast her fruit before the time in the field, saith the Lord of hosts" (Mal. 3:10, 11).

This promise is a challenge to everybody. The Lord says, "Prove Me." He is pleased when we believe and obey Him, and honored when we take Him at His Word. This Scripture is a challenge which gives us a legal right to prove Him. When a promise is made unto children on condition and they meet the condition, they remind their parents of their promise and expect them to keep their word. When we are faithful along all lines, specifically in the giving of tithes and offerings to the

Lord, when a need or emergency arises, whether physical, material, or spiritual, we may look up to the Lord and with courage and confidence ask the Lord for the desired blessing, saying, "Lord, my tithes and offerings have been joyfully given to Thee, now hear me and grant the petition to Thy servant." Such a claim upon the Lord will act as a great leverage in moving the Lord to grant our petition. The above promise is very practical to plead when in need, for the Lord loveth a cheerful giver.

II. Living in God's Purpose

"And we know that all things work together for good to them that love God, to them who are the called according to His purpose" (Rom. 8:28).

Some one has very aptly said, "God's promises hang over God's purposes." When we discover what God's purposes are for our lives, obey and love Him fervently, we may by faith appropriate all that is needful for us in the accomplishment of His purposes.

When we know that all things work together for good, that we love God, are called by Him, and are living in His purpose, these things give us courage, boldness, and faith in prayer. God, as it were, gives us the long end of the lever with the truth as a block to pry on. He gives us the advantage of the promises since we are weak, and He does the hard part, for He is infinite and omnipotent. He has given us many precious promises as encouragements and inducements to pray.

III. Courting God's Glory

"Now therefore let Me alone, that My wrath may wax hot against them, and that I may consume them: and I will make of thee a great nation" (Ex. 32:10).

Greatness is dangerous. Not many people can stand either great material prosperity or spiritual success. Gifts have a tendency to puff up, or to make the highly talented elated, which leads to self-trust, self-reliance, and pride. Pride goeth before destruction. Many great men have fallen through pride. When a person takes the glory to himself, he will lose the glory of God. The person who touches not the glory, neither seeks it, but leaves it alone, and seeks to glorify God, may ever rise higher. Moses was very meek; he sought no glory only to glorify God; therefore, he could move God and command Him so that God hearkened to his pleas. On one occasion God cried out to Moses, (Deity crying out to humanity) "Let Me alone." Moses did not leave God alone. He considered matters from God's viewpoint, sought God's glory and the good of others, being forgetful of himself, and employed that as a lever to move God, and God hearkened to him.

IV. Considering the Poor

"Blessed is he that considereth the poor: the Lord will deliver him in time of trouble. The Lord will preserve him, and keep him alive; and he shall be blessed upon the earth: and thou wilt not deliver him unto the will of his enemies. The Lord will strengthen him upon the bed of languishing: Thou wilt make all his bed in his sickness" (Ps. 41:1-3).

This Scripture is overlooked by many people. They do not know that it is in the Bible. If this condition is met when physical need arises, this promise is good to plead before the Lord, and it will act as a lever to move God. The Lord will bring deliverance in time of trouble. The Lord may well afford to preserve and keep alive such an one, for he is profitable to Him and to others. This Scripture, if practiced through life, will also be a comfort to people in the evening of life, when their sun will set. These will have an easier time in dying. Some people have a hard time, a struggle, in dying. They look back over their past lives, and it looks dark; but when they look into the future, it looks darker. They do not want to die and leave all their means to others. The Christian who has been generous, lived for others, has helped poor people in life, may plead this promise in sickness, and it will avail. In old age, when the hour comes for them to depart, they may look back, and all looks bright, then look forward, and all looks brighter, then die in peace, for their treasures have helped others, and at the same time have been laid up in heaven awaiting them, where they will enjoy them forever.

V. Seeking the Welfare of Others

"I say unto you, Though he will not rise and give him, because he is his friend, yet because of his importunity he will rise
and give him as many as he needeth. And I say unto you, Ask,
and it shall be given you; seek, and ye shall find; knock, and it
shall be opened unto you" (Luke 11:8, 9).

Every spiritual and aggressive Christian can come
with greater courage to the Lord, press a claim harder,
and exercise more faith when he comes to the Lord in
the behalf of others than he does when praying for
self. Such an attitude and motive serve as a lever to
move God to hearken. This truth is illustrated by the
parable of the importunate man. He could not have
pressed his claim as hard for himself as he did in behalf of another in need. The person who has not come to
the place where he can plead more powerfully for others
than for himself should carefully study this parable.
A few years ago an evangelist and missionary, who had
been greatly used by the Lord, had blood poison in the
hand. He called for other Christians to meet at his
house to unite with him in prayer for his healing. When
they gathered, the burden for sinners was a greater
concern to him than his healing. He made request that
all pray for sinners to become converted in the revival
which was then in progress. He, with others, prayed for
lost souls, and just incidentally asked the Lord to heal
him. The tenor of that prayer meeting was "others."
He began to amend immediately, and sinners were
converted.

VI. Walking Before God with a Perfect Heart

"Then Hezekiah turned his face toward the wall, and prayed
unto the Lord, and said, Remember now, O Lord, I beseech Thee,
how I have walked before Thee in truth and with a perfect heart,
and have done that which is good in Thy sight. And Hezekiah
wept sore" (Isa. 38:2, 3).

Isaiah, with a startling message from the Lord,
came to Hezekiah and told him to set his house in order
for he should die and not live. In his apparent dying
hours, Hezekiah desired to live longer; and he knew
that God was the only hope for his recovery, and could
give him a new lease on life. As a leverage for his

petition, he reminded the Lord that he had walked before Him with a perfect heart. His prayer availed and the Lord lengthened his life fifteen years. Walking before God in truth, with a perfect heart, and doing that which is right in His sight will have a great weight in moving God to answer our prayers. This is true in relation to praying for physical health, spiritual help, success in service, or for material blessings. Some Scriptures have a spiritual, a physical, and a material application; some an individual and a collective application; and some have a present and a future application. Then let us not forget, what God has done or promised to others is also applicable to us.

VII. Praying in the Line Christ has Made Request

"Therefore said He unto them, The harvest truly is great, but the laborers are few; pray ye therefore the Lord of the harvest, that He would send forth laborers into His harvest" (Luke 10:2).

Christ said, "After this manner therefore pray ye: Our Father which art in heaven, hallowed be Thy name. Thy kingdom come." The kingdom of God with the new heaven and new earth are certain to come. But we are co-workers with Him, and He allows us to work with Him, and has commanded us to pray to that end. Our prayers will help, and move the Lord to do that which He has promised and wants to do.

An illustration of this fact is the release of the Jews from the seventy years of captivity in Babylon. The Lord through Jeremiah predicted the seventy years of captivity and the release. God promised to accomplish this; however, He accomplished it through the prayers and influence of Daniel the prophet. God works through human instrumentality. In the evening of the seventy years of their captivity, Daniel studied the prophecies of Jeremiah and read the prediction of the release, and he became greatly concerned. His concern gave expression in prayer. In Daniel, chapter nine, we read Daniel's prayer. Knowing God's will, then praying in His will and for the accomplishment of His will, will act as a lever to move God to bring it to pass. We can always remind the Lord to do that which we know He has promised and those things we know He wants done.

It is the purpose of Christ to evangelize the world. However, we dare not take the attitude which an old preacher took in a ministerial meeting who had invited the younger ministers to propose a subject for discussion. There was no reply till at last William Carey suggested, "Whether the command given to the apostles to teach all nations, was not obligatory on all succeeding ministers to the end of the world, seeing that the accompanying promise was of equal extent." The aged chairman shouted out the rebuke: "Young man, that is none of our business. When God wants to evangelize the world, He will do it without your or my help. You are a miserable enthusiast for asking such a question. Certainly nothing can be done before another Pentecost, when an effusion of miraculous gifts, including the gift of tongues, will give effect to the commission of Christ as at first." Carey for the moment was greatly mortified. but his fervor did not cool off. He became the Father of Modern Missions.

The attitude for us to take is to recognize that He will evangelize the world through His followers, feel our individual responsibility, pray as though it all depended on our prayers, believe as if all depended on our faith, give as though it depended on our giving, then go as though it depended on our going. The person who does so is a true missionary. Of course, one person can not evangelize the whole world by himself; however, after he has done all these things, he may pray to the Lord of the harvest that He will send forth laborers into His harvest. This prayer will become a lever with which he may mightily move the Lord of the harvest that He will send forth many laborers into the harvest field. Since Christ has requested that we pray for this, it should encourage us to do so, which is a practical and positive manner of accomplishing much for the Lord's cause.

CHAPTER XIV

HOW GOD ANSWERS PRAYER

Some people are tempted that God does not answer prayer. Others say that God has answered the prayers of some people, but that He does not answer their prayers, for He answers only a few of the choicest of men and women. The fact remains that God does answer prayer. He will answer the prayers of any person who honestly and sincerely prays. God is no respecter of persons. When people meet conditions, He will answer their prayers. Let this fact be remembered that He answers every prayer in some manner, sometime, somewhere. If the prayers are not answered in the manner we want Him to answer, He will answer them in His own way, time, and place. If our prayers are not answered immediately, that is not sufficient reason to say that He does not answer our prayers.

I. God May Answer "Yes." If He Says "Yes," He has Given a Positive Answer to Our Prayer

"If ye shall ask anything in My name, I will do it" (John 14:14).

It is a joy to obtain answers to our prayers, and it is very gratifying when the Lord says "Yes," that is, gives a positive answer. The answer should be received very gratefully, and praise and thanksgiving offered unto Him. It also should draw us a little closer to Him. Every believer should expect answers to his prayers. It is "yes" answers that we should expect and strive after. When we pray for that which we need, which we know God wants to give us, which will glorify Him, and pray on scriptural ground and in faith, we will receive a "yes" answer and just what we have asked for in our prayer.

II. He May Answer "No." If He Says "No," He has Answered in a Negative Manner

"I pray Thee, let me go over, and see the good land that is beyond Jordan, that goodly mountain, and Lebanon. But the Lord was wroth with me for your sakes, and would not hear me: and the Lord said unto me, Let it suffice thee; speak no more unto Me of this matter" (Deut. 3:25, 26).

There was a reason known unto God why He did not say "Yes" to Moses. When God says "No" to our prayers, there is a reason for it. If He denies us, the fault is not with Him, but it is for our good. If He says "No," He has given an answer just the same. Then our attitude should be that of sweet submission and accept it joyfully. No complaint should be made. We should love and trust the Lord just the same. The Lord explained to Moses the reason He did not answer his prayer. The object of prayer is to get answers, "Yes" answers, and not "No" answers. No Christian should ever offer a prayer when he knows God will say "No." If he knows God does not want to grant his petition, such so-called praying is not real prayer. Such prayers could not be offered in faith, and whatsoever is not of faith is sin; therefore, it is presumptuous to offer such prayers. We need holy desires begotten of God, Bible promises, and faith to get "Yes" answers. Praying according to His will will obtain "Yes" answers. We need to know God's Word so that we may pray according to His will. If it is not His will to answer our prayer, why pray for it; rather ask for grace to do without. Pray for that which He wants us to have. Why should we want anything He does not want us to have? If we do, in that thing we are unlike Him.

III. God May Answer, "I Will Give You Something Better"

"For this thing I besought the Lord thrice, that it might depart from me. And He said unto me, My grace is sufficient for thee" (II Cor. 12:8, 9).

Paul besought the Lord three times to remove the thorn in his flesh. The Lord did not remove the thorn, but He gave him more grace. The thorn became an occasion for the Lord to bestow more grace on Paul, which made him more useful, and glorified God more. If the Lord says, "No, I will not give you that which you have asked, but I will give you something better," He has given us an answer to our prayer. God knows what is best for us, and will always do that which is best. In doing the better thing for us, He will have answered us definitely and gloriously.

IV. God May Answer, "You Wait a While." If He Says, "You Wait a While," He has Answered, and in Due Time He Will Grant the Petition in a Full Manner

"And shall not God avenge His own elect, which cry day and night unto Him, though He bear long with them?" (Lu. 18:7).

There are examples of this fact in the Bible. The Lord called Moses to lead Israel out of Egypt. It seemed that his prayers were being delayed, and he reminded the Lord that He had not made Pharaoh willing, nor Israel, who wanted Moses to leave them alone. The Lord dealt faithfully and patiently with Israel and Moses. Evidently it took Moses almost a year to get Israel out of Egypt. The remarkable fact is that on schedule time, in God's time, even the very selfsame day as God had predicted, He led them out. God always operates in the fulness of time. He is never late, nor does He act prematurely.

Another example of this fact was the birth of John the Baptist. The parents, Zacharias and Elisabeth, were childless, and had prayed for a son. To them it seemed God had said "No." They became old and stricken with age, gave up hope, and even forgot their prayers. God simply said, "You wait a while;" then in His own time He chose them to become the parents of John, the forerunner of Christ. The first thing the angel Gabriel said was, "Fear not, Zacharias: for thy prayer is heard." God set the time for the birth of John so that he would precede Christ by the space of six months.

Sometimes God tests us. He does so to see what we will do, how we will act, how much we love Him. He

may allow affliction to come, poverty, hunger, or a lack
of clothes. Then in due time He will graciously answer.
In this way He increases our faith and love.

Whenever we pray for people, we need to give the
Lord time to answer because men are creatures of time
and because the Lord will not coerce the wills of men.
He must make them willing. George Mueller of Bristol,
England, is considered as having been one of the greatest men of prayer and faith in this age. He prayed in
food and supplies before breakfast; however, he related that he prayed daily for two men over a period of
sixty years. That totaled almost twenty-two thousand
petitions. He died, and these two men were not yet
converted. The Lord did not answer his prayers until
after his death.

H. H. Dobney wrote the following on delays in answer to prayer: "Pa said he liked us to ask him for
whatever we wanted, and I asked him yesterday to get
me a kite, and he has not got it for me! said a curley-
headed grumbler, on a cold foggy day in November.
Yes, I asked him to give me a gold watch, and he has
never given me one! said a brother two or three years
older; and I don't see the good of asking for things. Six
months passed by, when behold; one fine day in May,
the father came in with a beautiful kite, which he gave
to his little boy without saying a word. But it was eight
or nine years before he called the other boy to him and
said, I suppose you have forgotten, when you were a
boy in pinafores, asking me for a gold watch, haven't
you? Yes, that I have, answered the now tall youth.
But I have not, said the father. Here's the watch, my
dear boy; you can value it and take care of it now! Ah,
Christian, need I add a word? else I might say that
prayers do not spoil by keeping, but are only put out
at interest." When God says, "You wait a while," we
can well afford to patiently await His appointed time.

V. God May Answer, "You Have Not Met the Right Conditions." If This is What He Said to Us, He has Answered and Waits Until We Meet the Right Conditions

"He that turneth away his ear from hearing the law, even his prayer shall be abomination" (Prov. 28:9).

Prayer is not merely asking the Lord for anything and everything we want. Getting answers to our prayers is not the mere receiving of everything we ask for. Prayer and answers are vastly more than these. Prayer is the earnest desire of the heart for the things God wants us to ask; and the answer is the receiving of those things God wants to give us, which we have asked for in His will. If we have not met the right conditions, God will not answer our prayers. For Him to do so would compromise His holiness, which He will never do. If God would answer our prayers when we have not met the right conditions, He would virtually say, "You may do as you please and have your own way and get anything you want." No, God will never do business with us when it compromises His holiness, or when we have not met the right conditions.

VI. God May Answer, "You Cherish an Idol in Your Heart and I Cannot Compromise My Holiness in Answering Your Prayer. When You Give up that Cherished Idol or Sin in Your Heart, Surrender and Repent, Then I Will Answer Your Prayer."

". . . and they went after other gods to serve them. . . . Therefore thus saith the Lord, Behold, I will bring evil upon them . . . and though they shall cry unto Me, I will not hearken unto them" (Jer. 11:10, 11).

God delights to be called upon, to be trusted, and for us to place our faith in Him, when we turn away from all sin. If He is honored as the true and living God, as the supreme One, and is given the supreme place in our lives, He will be pleased to prove to us that He is a rewarder of those who diligently seek Him. However, He is a jealous God, and will never give His honor to another. When prayers are not answered, the heart should be searched to see if anything is there which grieves the Lord. If anything is cherished more than He that will hinder prayer.

VII. God May Answer, "You Are Not Walking in the Light"

"But they refused to hearken, and pulled away the shoulder, and stopped their ears, that they should not hear. Therefore it is come to pass, that as He cried and they would not hear; so they cried, and I would not hear, saith the Lord of hosts" (Zech. 7:11, 13).

Why should God bless some people and answer their prayers? They are not walking in the light. Should God answer their prayers, He would endorse their worldliness, disobedience, and laxness. They would take it for granted that they were all right. The Lord will not place His approval on any who disobey Him. We cannot do as we please and get anything we want from Him. If we want what God has promised in His Word, we must obey what He has commanded in His Word.

CHAPTER XV

THE GREAT EXEMPLAR OF PRAYER

Christ is the Saviour of sinners and the Pattern for Christians. The apostle Peter was much with Christ and learned from Him. In his first Epistle he wrote that Christ left us an example that we should follow in His steps. Christ lived a holy and perfect life. He became a perfect Saviour and Substitute for all men. Yet, at the same time, He lived a life as the ideal Pattern, how a son of God should live. We do well to pattern after Him in His prayer life. Praying unto His Father constituted one of the main activities in the ministry of Christ. The word "pray" and "prayer" are employed twenty-five times in connection with the life and teachings of Christ while He was on earth.

I. Christ Prayed Before Entering into the Ministry

"Now when all the people were baptized, it came to pass, that Jesus also being baptized, and praying, the heaven was opened, and the Holy Ghost descended in a bodily shape like a dove upon Him, and a voice came from heaven, which said, Thou art My beloved Son; in Thee I am well pleased" (Lu. 3:21, 22).

We may well assume that Christ prayed much from His earliest childhood, and kept it up through His ministry, even praying while He was hanging on the cross. It is not stated what the subject of His prayer was when He stood on the brink of the Jordan River, but evidently the object was the reception and the anointing of the Holy Spirit on His humanity in order to empower Him as a Man to perform efficiently His earthly ministry and to accomplish redemption. Every person entering into the ministry should learn, experience, and practice the art of effective praying. Then he should even go farther than that, and pray for the baptism with the Holy Ghost to cleanse and empower him for holy living and efficient service.

II. Christ Arose Early in the Morning to Pray

"And in the morning, rising up a great while before day, He went out, and departed into a solitary place, and there prayed" (Mark 1:35).

Christ arose early, a great while before day, for a threefold purpose. It will be all the more interesting and inspiring when it is observed that the day before (Sabbath) had been a very busy day for Him. He had taught in the synagogue, performed miracles, such as casting out demons and going home with Simon Peter where He healed his mother-in-law of a fever. Then after the sun set, the entire city gathered at the door, and He performed miracles on a wholesale manner in which multitudes were healed. No doubt He retired at a late hour. Christ arose early the next morning, first, that He might be alone in quiet meditation, secondly, to commune with His Father in prayer, and thirdly, that He might receive the anointing and power upon Him as a Man, to prepare Him for the new duties of a new day. To pray well, we must pray early. Christians must choose between indulging in a little more sleep with time for prayer cut short and a scant but hurried devotion, or a little self-denial in sleep with the best and first part of the day given to God. Christ had no conveniences to pray, but He made them.

III. Christ Continued all Night in Prayer to God

"And it came to pass in those days, that He went out into a mountain to pray, and continued all night in prayer to God" (Luke 6:12).

Christ was an itinerate Preacher; He journeyed from place to place. Unlike traveling men today who travel from city to city, whose first concern in coming to a new town is to seek a restaurant and something to eat and drink, and a hotel where they may stay for the night, Christ was concerned to find a mountain, or a solitary place, where He could go to pray. Instead of making eating and drinking His first and great concern, He made prayer His first great concern. Many people, when in a strange place, neglect prayer, and do not pray as much as when they are at home; however, Christ kept up His prayer life while He traveled. To Him a mountain became an ideal place to pray, and to be alone with His Father was a supreme delight.

IV. Christ Prayed and Blessed the Food Before Meals

"And He commanded the multitude to sit down on the grass, and took the five loaves, and the two fishes, and looking up to heaven, He blessed, and brake, and gave the loaves to His disciples, and the disciples to the multitude" (Matt. 14:19).

In blessing the food and thanking His Father for it, Christ left all of His followers a good example. Food is a good gift from God, and a physical necessity. Man is dependent on God for food. It is God Who gives the increase. He is the Giver of every good gift (material blessings) and all perfect gifts (spiritual blessings). Since man is dependent on God for his food, and God is the great Giver of food, man should very gratefully thank God for his food.

V. Christ Prayed Before and After Great Achievements in His Ministry

"When Jesus therefore perceived that they would come and take Him by force, to make Him a king, He departed again into a mountain Himself alone" (John 6:15).

Some people pray before great emergencies and achievements in life, but forget or neglect to pray and praise God afterward. It is just as righteous and as essential to pray and praise God after great victories and achievements as it is to pray beforehand. To do so will be a safeguard against becoming self-satisfied, self-reliant, powerless, and being unprepared for the next emergency. It also leads to humility of heart and greater achievements in the future. Christ prayed after great achievements as well as before. He went from victory to victory and from success to success. He was always prayed up-to-date. It was essential for Christ to pray much that He might have the power of the Spirit resting on Him as a Man for the accomplishment of His ministry. He was never below par, or unprepared to meet the emergencies of life.

VI. Christ Prayed Much When He Was Unusually Busy

"But so much the more went there a fame abroad of Him: and great multitudes came together to hear, and to be healed by Him of their infirmities. And He withdrew Himself into the wilderness, and prayed" (Luke 5:15, 16).

The more busy some people become, the less they pray. They take time to work, to eat, and to sleep. Prayer is sacrificed and neglected. Sometimes Christ was so busy that He did not find time to eat, rest, or sleep, but He took time to pray, even if He had to do without eating or sleeping. Increased work did not crowd out His praying time. He knew how to discipline Himself in relation to His time and labors so that prayer was never neglected. O, that we might be more like Him! Great results followed after He had been alone in communion with His Father. That prepared Him to again appear in public.

VII. Christ Prayed for Others

"And the Lord said, Simon, Simon, behold, Satan hath desired to have you, that he may sift you as wheat: but I have prayed for thee, that thy faith fail not" (Luke 22:31, 32).

"I pray not that Thou shouldest take them out of the world, but that Thou shouldest keep them from the evil" (John 17:15).

"Then said Jesus, Father, forgive them; for they know not what they do" (Luke 23:34).

Christ not only prayed for Himself, but He prayed for others. He prayed for Simon that his faith would not fail, and that Satan would not get him as he had Judas. Christ prayed for His disciples, as recorded in John seventeen. He also prayed for His enemies while He was hanging on the cross. This was not a vain prayer; He really meant it, for that was the very purpose for which He died on the cross. Most certainly some of the men who crucified Him were converted. We read in Acts that many of the priests became obedient to the faith. Peter preached saying, "Ye have taken, and by wicked hands have crucified and slain" Christ. Many of these became converted.

The order in the prayer life of Christ is interesting and profitable for us to consider and practice. He began

His ministry by praying for Himself and concluded it in praying for others. Others were His great concern. As the Son of God He was holy, and did not need to pray for Himself to become better; but He prayed for Himself that He might become more useful. We should pray for ourselves that we may become holy and useful, and for others that they may become holy and useful also.

CHAPTER XVI

A MODEL PRAYER

The prayer which Christ taught His disciples in Matthew 6:9-13, is commonly called The Lord's Prayer. It could be more properly called, The Disciples' Prayer, or The Model Prayer. This is a model prayer for all Christian people. Christ said, "After this manner therefore pray ye." The Lord did not intend for this prayer to become a ritual, or that people should become ritualistic in offering it. It is well for people to pray this prayer in faith, in truth, and in the spirit. This is not a prayer to be offered by sinners. The sinner can not call God, "Father." Neither is he in a condition to pray for others. He can only pray in a limited manner, that is, for himself, that God will be merciful to him and pardon him. This prayer teaches the "manner" and the "matter" of prayer. The scope of this prayer is astonishingly large. It includes the present and the future. It implies Christian experience, and assumes many doctrines. It teaches how broad a Christian's prayer life may and should be.

I. Worshiping in Spirit and Truth

"Our Father Which art in heaven, hallowed be Thy name" (v. 9).

"Our Father" implies that God is a Trinity and that He has a Son. It also implies the new birth and adoption, which are the means of sinners becoming sons of God. A sinner cannot call God his Father, for he does not have any such claim on God. He must be born again before he can address God as Father. The universal fatherhood of God and brotherhood of men are not taught in the Scriptures, but are a false hope many entertain. The doctrine of adoption implies the heirship and inheritance we have in Christ. Then the term, "Our Father," speaks of a near and dear relationship that the sons of God sustain to God, which gives them many privileges and a glorious right to come to Him, and of His love and care for His own. It is the nature of God as our Father to give good gifts to His children, especially the Holy Spirit, if they ask Him to do so. "Which art in heaven" teaches His Deity and supremacy, that there is a heaven for His children who some day will be with Him, and therefore, that there also must be a hell for all the wicked. "Thy name," implies His nature and attributes of holiness, omnipotence, omnipresence, omniscience, and that He is to be feared, revered, and worshiped.

II. Coming of God's Kingdom
"Thy kingdom come" (v. 10).

Christ commands here that we pray for the coming of God's kingdom. The kingdom of God will be supreme and eternal. There are many kingdoms. Satan has his kingdom; the world has its kingdoms; and Christ will have His kingdom some day. The kingdom of God will be the final, eternal, and the only kingdom which will be over all. It will come, and we should pray for its coming. Much is implied in its coming. Before its coming there are many events which must come to pass to make way for the coming of God's kingdom. Some of the great events which must come to pass before God's kingdom will come are the completion of the church, the rapture and first resurrection, the tribulation judgments, the chaining of Satan, the Millennial kingdom, the resurrection and judgment of all the wicked, the eternal banishment of Satan and all his followers of demons and men into the lake of fire, and the renovation of the earth, out of which will come a new earth; then Christ will submit and emerge His kingdom into the kingdom of God, in order that Deity may reign with supremacy throughout eternity.

III. Eternal Righteousness in the Earth
"Thy will be done in earth, as it is in heaven" (v. 10).

When God's kingdom has come, with all sinners, Satan, and the wicked spirits banished, with all rebellion brought in subjection, and all traces of sin forever removed, then eternal righteousness will reign; sin will never break out, and God's will will be done on earth just as it is done in heaven. What a blessed time that will be! May God hasten that time! This is what the Christian should pray for, then work for its coming. There was a sinless past, and there will come a sinless future. Then there will not be any sin, curses, sorrows, tears, heartaches, deaths, or separations. Let us pray for the coming of God's kingdom.

IV. Daily Physical Needs

"Give us this day our daily bread" (v. 11).

From the great spiritual, literal, and eternal issues and realities, for which we should pray, Christ then directs us to pray for our daily physical and temporal needs. We are dependent on our heavenly Father for our daily physical needs, as well as our spiritual, heavenly, and eternal blessings. God is mindful of our daily needs, our bread, which we eat. This is to become an object of our daily prayers. However, this is to be prayed for just a day at a time. We cannot pray for tomorrow's necessities, even as we cannot eat today for tomorrow's strength and hunger. Our dependence is on God for our daily physical needs, as well as our spiritual blessings.

V. Tenderness of Heart

"And forgive us our debts, as we forgive our debtors" (v. 12).

When the Christian has done his best, he still is an unprofitable servant of the Lord, and comes far short of absolute perfection. Heart perfection is possible; and the Lord looks upon the heart, and accepts the desires and motives of the heart when they are pure and holy. The very best people owe God moral and spiritual debts. The shortcomings of Christian people are atoned for by Christ. Christ freely forgives all who repent; therefore, all Christians should freely forgive others who do them an injustice. Christ taught us to have a forgiving spirit and to forgive freely, without any limit, or as often as a brother may sin against us, even unto "seventy times seven" in one day. Every Christian will do well to seek pardon for his failures and shortcomings, and to pray for a tender and compassionate heart.

VI. Victory in Spiritual Conflict

"And lead us not into temptation, but deliver us from evil" (v. 13).

This petition has puzzled many people and troubled others. To them it seems to reveal God as an active agent in subjecting us to temptation. From James 1:13 we learn that this is not so. In Luke 22:40 Christ admonished the three disciples by saying, "Pray that ye enter not into temptation." That may be the idea of verse thirteen. God tests people, or allows them to be tried, but not with an evil intent. No person should court or challenge temptations. Peter challenged testing and fell. Plenty of trials and sorrows come to all good people without courting them. The evil from which we should pray to be delivered, may refer to the Evil One, that is, the Devil, to evil men who may seek to do us harm, or to temptations which may lead us into sin. We may well pray, "And lead us not into temptation, but deliver us from evil," that we may overcome all temptations.

VII. Supremacy of Deity Through Eternity

"For thine is the kingdom, and the power, and the glory, for ever. Amen" (v. 13).

This model prayer closes with a doxology. The honor and praise ascribed to God is threefold. His kingdom will be endless; His power will be supreme through eternity; and His glory will be for ever. God is a great King, and His kingdom will be shared with His own. Should His kingdom have an end, that fact would mar the joy of the saints; but to know it will be endless, will make the joy of the saints full and complete. His power will be over all, and be revealed in ever increasing manifestations which will continue age after age. The

Father's glory is so great He will share it with His
redeemed children who in return will glorify Him,
which will create an ever increasing stream of blessing.
This will continue through eternity. Surely prayer
is a great ministry, and the Christian has great objectives for which to pray.

CHAPTER XVII

TEACHINGS OF CHRIST ON PRAYER

Christ is the Savior of sinners and the Pattern for Christians. His ministry was twofold. He saved, healed, and helped people directly; then He left an example how all of His followers should live and labor. The teachings of Christ on prayer are explicit, positive, instructive, and profitable. All that Christ has said concerning prayer should be studied and carefully considered, because He is the One Who answers our prayers. He said, "If ye abide in Me, and My words abide in you, ye shall ask what ye will, and it shall be done unto you" (John 15:7). When we abide in Him and His words abide in us, what we ask in prayer is as if He Himself had asked those things. More emphasis needs to be laid on the words of Christ. We should acquaint ourselves with His Word, particularly what He has said about prayer. His Word should be read, accepted, obeyed, and made a part of our lives. Those who are taught by Christ and obey His Word pray the best.

I. Praying in Christ's Name

"And whatsoever ye shall ask in My name, that will I do, that the Father may be glorified in the Son" (John 14:13).

It is well and proper to address our prayers, or conclude them, by saying, "In the name of Christ." "In the name of Christ" is vastly more than saying the words as a formula. We can pray in His name without saying the formula. When we say "in the name of Christ," it should be so in reality, in deeds, in belief, in spirit, as well as in words. "In My name" is equivalent to, "for My sake," or "on My account." Name also stands for nature. To pray in the name of Christ is to pray with His very nature and life in us. It involves a union and relationship with Christ as a woman to a man in marriage, in which she becomes one with him by taking his name as her name. It is like the union of a branch in the vine. If we want to employ the name of Christ in prayer, we need to be engaged in His work, and it must be for His cause and glory. To pray in His name is like filling in the amount in a check which is endorsed by His very signature. All that we ask in His name He will do, and all He does glorifies the Father.

II. Praying in Faith

"And all things, whatsoever ye shall ask in prayer, believing, ye shall receive" (Matt. 21:22).

This is a great and gracious promise. It includes "all things" and "whatsoever." Christ waits on our asking. He wants us to ask Him, for He has much to give us. Some one has said, "The Lord wants many customers who come unto Him often and that will take away much." One writer says, "Prayer is the bow, the promise is the arrow; faith is the hand which draws the bow, and sends the arrow with the heart's message to heaven. The bow without the arrow is of no use, and the arrow without the bow is of little worth, and both without the strength of the hand are to no purpose. Neither the promise without prayer, nor prayer without the promise, nor both without faith avail the Christian anything. What was said of the Israelites, 'They could not enter in, because of unbelief,' the same may be said of many of our prayers; they cannot enter heaven, because they are not put up in faith."

III. Praying in the Atonement

"If ye shall ask any thing in My name, I will do it" (John 14:14.)

The question, Is it included in the atonement?, is often asked, as though some things come as a benefit of Christ's death, and others merely by the will of the Lord, or our own merits. Every answer to our prayers and every blessing we receive, whether material or spiritual, such as salvation, victory, grace, healing, money, clothes, wisdom, deliverance, etc., all come, not as a result of our own merits, but as a result of the death of Jesus Christ. His death paid it all. By the death of Christ, He has accumulated an infinite fund of merit. When we pray we should place the value of Christ's blood on the privilege of prayer, the prayer itself, and on the expectation of the answer. When we ask in His name, it is as if He Himself had asked for those things; therefore, He will make it good. To pray in the atonement, we must be careful to obey every law of God, and be willing to know and do His will. To pray in the atonement, is to ask for those things which Christ died to bring to pass. We are not to misuse this means for any selfish motive. Prayer is not a weapon with which we can compel Deity to gratify our bigotry, or selfish whims. A woman prayed (said some words) all night long that the Lord would keep her husband from joining a certain church. Her motive was personal and selfish. This was not praying in the atonement.

One minister said to another, "Brother ——, I have been praying for you all night long."

"That was fine. I appreciate your praying for me. And why did you pray for me all night long?" enquired the other minister.

"That God," said he, "would lead you to join our denomination."

"I do not call that praying at all. You might just as well have gone to bed and slept all night," replied he. Praying, to be effective, needs to be in the promise and purpose of the Lord, and for the purpose for which He died and for His glory, and not for any selfish motive.

IV. Praying in the Will of God

"And He went a little farther, and fell on His face, and prayed, saying, O My Father, if it be possibe, let this cup pass from Me: nevertheless not as I will, but as Thou wilt" (Matt. 26:39).

The greatest delight of Christ was to do the will of His Father. It was more pleasing to Him than life. He was willing to die in order to please His Father. We should never strive to bring God to our will, but His will should become our will. True prayer will bring our will in subjection to the will of God. Being able to pray to the point which will make us forget our own will and leave all in His hands, or that our will merge into His will, is true praying. When we submit to the will of God, we make the best progress. All of our prayers should be submitted to the will of our heavenly Father.

V. Praying Without Ceasing

"And He spake a parable unto them to this end, that men ought always to pray, and not to faint" (Luke 18:1).

We should pray without ceasing because God wills it, duty demands it, and the need requires it. The Christian's recourse is prayer and his resource is God. This is sufficient. Right here is where many people fail, that is, they do not utilize their recourse and God's resource. Praying is the lifetime duty and privilege of every Christian. "Always to pray," is never to cease to pray. It is to be in a perpetual attitude of prayer. It is always to pray as we always eat, as we always sleep, as we always arise in the morning, or as we always go to work. It is to be ready to pray any instant, to be as regular as we are with any good habit or duty. "Not to faint" is a military term. It means never to abandon anything because of cowardice, hardships, inconveniences, laziness, suffering, or discouragement. God's people are to continue to pray until victory comes, until they receive what they ask for in God's will .The thought is continuity, persistence, and perseverance. The parable Christ gave concerning the widow and the unjust judge illustrates some great principles and truths in prayer. The unjust judge, who feared not God nor regarded men, was an expression of a selfish, careless, unprincipled character, and in this he contrasts with God. We learn that God is just and willing, that He possesses power and wisdom. He will hear and deliver His own. The widow, who was oppressed, represents the Christian people in this world; and the adversary represents Satan, who tempts, oppresses, and afflicts God's people. The widow came, that is, she kept coming. She came once and again and again to the unjust and unwilling judge. If he, being unjust and unwilling, could be moved by her continual coming, how much more certain will Christ our just and willing Judge answer our prayers when we importune!

VI. Praying in Unity

"I say unto you, That if two of you shall agree on earth as touching any thing that they shall ask, it shall be done for them of My Father which is in heaven. For where two or three are gathered together in My name, there am I in the midst of them" (Matt. 18:19, 20).

This is a challenging promise. Man's "if" will be met by Christ's "shall." The condition is for two or three to meet in His name and agree as touching any thing. Experience and observation teach us the virtue of "praying bands," "company praying," or "united praying." Christ interceded alone, and much of our interceding must be done alone; however, He also taught that there should be united praying. Two or three are the least numbers which may agree and meet in unity. This is encouraging, for had He said two or three thousand it would be nigh impossible to get that many people together for a prayer meeting. In His name, is to meet in His nature and for His glory. Christ is the Mediator between God and men. He is the only means of approach to God. When He is given His rightful place, He will meet with His own. The divine presence is essential to prayer. This promise teaches the omnipresence of Christ and assures the omnipotence of Christ.

VII. Praying With Holy Desires

"Therefore I say unto you, What things soever ye desire, when ye pray, believe that ye receive them, and ye shall have them" (Mark 11:24).

The heart has the capacity for great desires. Holy desires come from a holy heart that is regulated by a holy will. Then desires arise out of the heart as we cherish what the Lord wants to give. Holy desires become intensified as we cherish them. Holy desires also are inspired by the Holy Spirit, Who operates in our hearts and moves on us to ask for the things the Lord wants to give us, or do through us; and God looks into the heart when we pray. He measures our desires. Desire is an essential element in prayer. To pray without a desire is mockery. Where there is no desire of the heart, we are not moved, and that will not move God, for He looks into the heart. Again, where there is no desire, there will be no emotion, no faith; neither would there be any appreciation or gratitude should the prayer be answered. Without desires we are limited in our praying. Where there is an intense desire, it will help us to plead as if it were for our eternal destiny and the destinies of others. Such desires coupled with faith will be honored and answered.

CHAPTER XVIII

INTERCESSORY PRAYER

Intercession is prayer, but all praying is not intercession. Intercession is one type of prayer. It is the petitioning, or entreating in behalf of another, or others. Not all of our prayers should be bestowed on ourselves. It is not sin nor selfishness to pray for ourselves. It would be well for all people if they would pray more for themselves. If they would do so, they could pray better for others. It is scriptural to pray for ourselves; however, if we pray only for ourselves and fail to pray for others, we are not Christ-like in this, and are greatly lacking in our prayer lives. We need to pray for others, for they also need it. The ministry of intercession is one of the greatest ministries. This is the ministry of a third party bringing two parties together, even God and man. Somebody prayed for us before we were converted; therefore, we owe it to others who do not pray for themselves, that they may be converted; then they will be in a condition to pray for themselves and also for others. The sinners are not the only ones who need our prayers, but those who have been converted that they may be preserved from evil. All servants of the Lord need the prayers of others.

I. For All Men

"I exhort therefore, that, first of all, supplications, prayers, intercessions, and giving of thanks, be made for all men" (I Tim. 2:1).

All men should be prayed for, because all men do not pray for themselves. Christ died for all and salvation has been provided for all; therefore, all may be saved. Satan works to deceive all men and to keep them in sin. All unsaved people are prospects for personal workers. Most certainly every saved person was converted through the prayers and influence of some one else. It is the duty of Christian people to pray for the unsaved all around them that the Lord will save them.

II. For Those Who Are in Authority

"For kings, and for all that are in authority; that we may lead a quiet and peaceable life in all godliness and honesty" (I Tim. 2:2).

The saintly people will be positively benefited in praying for those in authority, and so will the political officers. Those in authority need to be converted, and may be converted if they are being prayed for. Satan works in different ways to offset and to hinder the progress of the gospel. Some ways in which Satan works against the cause of Christ are: by controlling the governmental powers, which would bring about a corrupt state religion, by uniting the church and the state, by preventing religious liberty and closing the doors to gospel workers, and by allowing the persecution of gospel workers. Examples of these facts have been the rulers of some nations in the past. Their rule has brought much persecution, sorrow, closed churches, and martyrdom. Satan works in high places, that is, the seats of government in every country. Kings, and those in authority, are officers to maintain order and peace, to punish the guilty, and to protect the innocent. Prayer needs to be offered for all in authority that Satan will be restrained in deceiving rulers and that they may rule righteously and justly. While gospel workers enjoy religious liberty and national protection, they should be thankful to God and aggressively spread the gospel. Many people fail to pray for their rulers. Instead of praying for them they speak evil of them. When President W. G. Harding died on August 2, 1923, a Christian woman heard her telephone ring. When she answered the call and was informed that the President had died suddenly, she confessed that as soon as she heard the news her heart was smitten with guilt because she had failed to pray for him as the Scriptures commanded. Very evidently she was not the only person who felt guilty along that line. No doubt many who heard on April 12, 1945, of the sudden death of President Roosevelt, felt condemnation for having failed to pray for him. Though rulers may not be all they should be, or that Christians think they should be, that becomes a reason we should pray for them.

III. For Our Enemies

"Love your enemies, bless them that curse you, do good to them that hate you, and pray for them which despitefully use you, and persecute you" (Matt. 5:44).

There are several reasons why we should pray for our enemies. (1) Christ commanded it and that makes it a privilege. (2) It is scriptural and that makes it a responsibility. (3) They need to be prayed for because they are lost. (4) It is a Christlike spirit. Christ prayed for His enemies that they might be forgiven. (5) It will help us to love them. (6) It may lead to an occasion in which we may do good to them and thereby win them. (7) Then God will begin to move on them, and conviction will come to them, which may lead to their salvation. (8) It may lead them to become our friends; then they will cease to hate or persecute us.

IV. For the Sick

"Is any sick among you? let him call for the elders of the church; and let them pray over him, anointing him with oil in the name of the Lord . . . Confess your faults one to another, and pray one for another, that ye may be healed" (James 5:14-16).

There are several conditions stipulated by the Lord which enter into the healing of the sick. These are: calling of the elders, praying over the sick, anointing the sick with oil, prayer of faith and confessing faults one to another. The sick need to be prayed for, because when a person is sick he may die; and if he is unsaved and dies in that state, he will be eternally lost. Praying for the sick has led to the salvation of many. Then when a person who is a Christian is sick, he can not be as fervent, as aggressive, and as earnest in prayer as he can when he is healthy. He needs the prayers of the Christian people.

V. For Israel

"Moreover as for me, God forbid that I should sin against the Lord in ceasing to pray for you: but I will teach you the good and the right way" (I Sam. 12:23).

"Brethren, my heart's desire and prayer to God for Israel is, that they might be saved" (Rom. 10:1).

"For I am not ashamed of the gospel of Christ: for it is the power of God unto salvation to every one that believeth; to the Jew first, and also to the Greek" (Rom. 1:16).

The Lord said to Abraham, "I will bless them that bless thee, and curse him that curseth thee." This promise is true today, even as it has been from the time the Lord uttered it. All who say "It is good luck to curse a Jew" are sadly mistaken. On the other hand, Christian people would court the favor of the Lord if they would pray for Israel that they might be saved. It was Paul's policy to preach to the Jews first, wherever he went. Nothing would be lost, but much would be gained, if the policy "to the Jews first" were practiced by Christian people in their praying, preaching, and giving. J. Hudson Taylor, the founder of the China Inland Mission, made it his policy on the first day of each year to write out a check for the evangelization of the Jews. This would be a good practice for all Christians to follow, then they would be led to pray for them.

VI. For All Saints

"Praying always with all prayer and supplication in the Spirit, and watching thereunto with all perseverance and supplication for all saints" (Eph. 6:18).

Christian people owe a special obligation to other Christians. The mistake many church people make is they put forth a great effort in getting sinners into church services and revival meetings, pray, weep, and entreat them to seek Christ, then, when they are converted, neglect them, show little interest in them, care not whether they attend prayer meeting or Sunday services, and forget to pray for them. Christians owe obligations to sinners, but their obligations are even greater to fellow Christians. Paul writes, "As we have therefore opportunity, let us do good unto all men, especially unto them who are of the household of faith." James admonishes us to "pray one for another."

VII. For Ministers

"Ye also helping together by prayer for us" (II Cor. 1:11).

"Praying always . . . and for me, that utterance may be given unto me, that I may open my mouth boldly, to make known the mystery of the gospel" (Eph. 6:18, 19).

Practically all church members are greatly failing along one line of duty, that is, to pray for ministers, pastors, and evangelists. Probably most church members think that these out of all peoples do not need the prayers of the people. However, ministers are the one class that need to be prayed for more than any other. We think that sinners need to be prayed for more than any other people. The Bible does not lay as great stress on praying for sinners as it does that sinners be preached to. The Old Testament prophets preached repentance to the ungodly in Zion. John the Baptist, Christ, the apostles, and Paul preached repentance to their congregations. The heathen could be prayed for all their lives, but that would not save them or lead them to believe in Christ. When the gospel is preached to them, it will inspire faith in Christ which will lead to their salvation. More prayers need to be offered for pastors, evangelists, and missionaries that they may preach more effectively, powerfully, and scripturally. This will be the means of more people hearing the gospel, which produces conviction for sins and inspires faith in Christ. Church members, pray more for your pastor and evangelist. This will bear fruit in their ministry, for the divinely ordained method of saving people is through the preaching of the gospel. The church at Antioch prayed for Barnabas and Paul as they were sent forth. Throughout his Epistles, Paul requested prayer that he might have open doors, boldness to preach the gospel, and for release from his bonds so that he might go forth to preach.

CHAPTER XIX

INTERCESSORY PRAYER OF DANIEL

Daniel was a man of prayer. He made prayer the first and the greatest business of his life. He was very regular in praying three times daily. Not only did he pray for himself, but he prayed for his own nation, the Jews. In Daniel, chapter nine, there is recorded the intercessory prayer of that saintly prophet who bore the burden of the whole nation. This is a very good example of an intercessory prayer. It was when Daniel studied the prophecies of Jeremiah and learned that the captivity of the Jews in Babylon should be seventy years, which then had almost run their course, that he became greatly concerned that something should be done about it. Certainly, it was the prayers of Daniel that moved God to release the Jews from their captivity.

I. Concern for Prayer

"In the first year of his reign I Daniel understood by books the number of the years, whereof the word of the Lord came to Jeremiah the prophet, that He would accomplish seventy years in the desolations of Jerusalem" (Daniel 9:2).

In order to offer an intercessory prayer, there must be a need on the part of another, or others, and a concern on the part of self, or the one burdened to intercede in behalf of the other party. The concern comes by knowing the need or crisis of others. When Daniel understood by books that the eve of the release was at hand, and no steps, or move, had been made about the Jews returning, he was startled and became greatly concerned. He knew that the only way this would come to pass was to pray it to pass. Some might say, "Well, if the Lord predicted that the captivity should continue only seventy years, why become concerned about it?

Why not let Him bring it to pass without any man becoming burdened for it?" The Lord works through human instrumentality, and He knew that Daniel would pray that event to pass. For that very purpose the Lord prepared Daniel, that when the occasion came, he as intercessor would pray it to pass.

II. Seeking God's Face and Favor

"I set my face unto the Lord God" (Dan. 9:3a).

This was an attitude of prayer and a preparation for prayer. In talking to people we want to see their faces, and they want to see our face. It would be strange and unnatural to visit a person to seek a favor, then each turn his back to the other one. When we seek a favor from one superior, we enter into his presence, and with our face observe him and wait until he with his face gives us his attention, then our request is made known. Some hurry into the presence of the Lord without any meditation, heart preparation, or patience, and hurriedly rattle off a prayer, then hurry away without seeing if the prayer secured the attention of God, and do not even wait for the answer. This is as if one person would hurriedly enter a grocery store, and without securing the attention of the grocer, place an order of fifteen different items, and then hurry out without paying for anything or waiting to receive them, then wonder why no groceries are obtained. God can give attention unto all people at the same time who honestly and humbly seek His face. Daniel set his face toward the Lord, and sought the face of the Lord. This means that he, as it were, set the face of the Lord before him, then set himself as in His presence, then as a face to face ordeal he prayed to the Lord.

III. Making His Request Known

"To seek by prayer" (Dan. 9:3b).

Prayer is talking to God. It is the general address unto God. Daniel knew that the Jews had sinned and greatly insulted God, and that repentance and confession needed to be made to the Lord to court His favor and grace in their release. In this prayer Daniel prayed as a priest, getting between God and the people, then, as it were, prayed vicariously, assuming all the sins of the Jews, confessing them before the Lord in their behalf. Such is intercessory prayer. The burdened saint, in a sense, assumes the place and the responsibility of the needy ones for whom he prays.

IV. Pressing His Entreaties
"And supplications" (Dan. 9:3b).

Supplications mean pressing entreaties. Daniel was greatly burdened and concerned for his people, their release and God's purposes concerning them. He pressed, or crowded, not merely his own claims, but the needs of the Jewish nation and God's claims. Because they were God's claims, he could pray in the plan of God. This gave him great courage and boldness. He had a just claim on God; therefore, he could justly press those claims, and become urgent in doing so. His prayer greatly pleased the Lord, and endeared him to all heaven. When the angel Gabriel came to enlighten him, he addressed Daniel as, "O man greatly beloved."

V. Fasting Instead of Feasting
"With fasting" (Dan. 9:3c).

This was the letting go of the physical necessities. He was more concerned about God's business than his own, about God's people than himself, about spiritual things than physical necessities. Eating is one of the greatest physical pleasures and belongs to the natural realm. Many people see to it that they have plenty to eat, even though they do not obtain much else in life. Most people are so thoroughly habituated to eating three times a day, they will eat when not hungry, or when sick. Daniel wanted deliverance for God's people more than he desired food. Fasting gave him more time to pray, and enabled him to be in a better state to pray. A saint can pray better with an empty stomach than with a full stomach.

VI. Humbling Himself Before God

"And sackcloth and ashes" (Dan. 9:3d).

This great intercessor put on sackcloth, and lay in the ashes to affect himself and his God. Taking such a lowly and humble attitude before the Lord greatly moved the loving heart of God. The better a person is in the sight of the Lord, when he humbles himself, the more it will move Him. Daniel was greatly beloved in heaven, and when he humbled himself before the Lord, the Lord could not deny His obedient servant.

VII. Confessing Israel's Sins

"And I prayed unto the Lord my God, and made my confession" (Dan. 9:4a).

Daniel was not a sinner, nor a backslider, neither a cold or formal professor. He was a devout saint of God who became an intercessor for a nation that had failed to confess its sins before God; therefore, Daniel, a holy man, took that place and confessed the iniquities, sins, and idolatries of the Jews and Jerusalem. This prayer greatly moved the Lord so that He hearkened to Daniel. Daniel prayed through before he was through praying. The answer came before he came to the "Amen." Gabriel, God's messenger, was sent to enlighten Daniel, and not only assure him of the release of the Jews from Babylon, but to give him a revelation of the future restoration and the establishment of the Messianic kingdom. The effects of intercessory prayer are greater and the number who are benefited by it is larger than the average person realizes. The need for intercessors is great. Who will qualify?

CHAPTER XX

PRAYER CHANGES THINGS

The Lord spoke through the prophet Jeremiah, saying, "Before they call, I will answer." There are times when the Lord sends the answer on the way before the petition is offered in prayer. God knows beforehand that some petitions are going to be offered, and the answer is imperative; therefore, He sends the answer on the way so it will arrive in due time. There have also been occasions in which God answered so instantly that the answer arrived before the offerer said "Amen." Seven examples are selected from Bible characters, showing that sometimes God answers prayer instantly, and that great changes were wrought in answer to their prayers. From these examples we learn that these changes came to pass in direct answer to their prayers. Many things will never come to pass unless we pray them to pass, and could we only know it, many things have not come to pass because we have not prayed. What is meant by the expression "Prayer Changes Things" is not that prayer in itself does the changing, but that God, to Whom prayer is offered, is moved by the prayer of faith and brings the changes to pass.

I. Job's Three Friends Were Converted and He Was Healed

"And the Lord turned the captivity of Job, when he prayed for his friends: also the Lord gave Job twice as much as he had before" (Job 42:10).

Here we learn that prayer will do what silence, argument, contention, criticism, and talking can not do. It was when God spoke and all (Job and his three friends) became silent that the Lord told them what to do. The three friends were commanded to bring their sacrifices, which was a confession that they were worthy of death and needed a substitute to find forgiveness, and Job, though full of boils, was told to pray for them. Several things took place while Job prayed: The Lord accepted the prayer of Job: He converted the three friends; the storm ended and the funnel of the tornado lifted and disappeared: the bonds of Satan were loosed and Job was instantly healed; Satan was defeated and silenced; Job was vindicated, and the Lord turned the captivity of Job. Some scholars teach that the turning of the captivity was the returning of his oxen and asses stolen by the Sabeans and the camels by the Chaldeans. Anyway, the great lesson we learn is that more can be done through prayer than by doing anything else.

II. The Death Sentence for Hezekiah Was Changed

"Then he turned his face to the wall, and prayed. . . . And it came to pass, afore Isaiah was gone out into the middle court, that the word of the Lord came to him, saying, turn again, and tell Hezekiah the captain of My people, Thus saith the Lord, the God of David thy father, I have heard thy prayer, I have seen thy tears: behold, I will heal thee" (II Kings 20:2-5).

Hezekiah was sick unto death. The Lord sent Isaiah to him with the startling message that he should set his house in order, for he would die and not live. If this death sentence is changed it must be changed by prayer. Hezekiah turned his face toward the wall, prayed, and wept. This good king was unwilling to die, for he was the captain of God's people in the midst of a great revival, in a great conflict against the Assyrians, and did not yet have a successor. His prayer was well ordered and worded. It was full of fervor, life, piety, affection, and humility. It also was full of tears. This prayer was pleasing to the Lord. His prayer went through and the answer came instantly. Isaiah had not gone out of the inner court when the Lord told him to return and tell Hezekiah that the Lord would heal him and add fifteen years to his life. If Hezekiah had not prayed, certainly he would have died. This should be an encouragement to us to pray at all times, to live righteously; then it will help our prayers and faith to move God in time of trouble, and it will also be a great inducement for God to answer our prayers.

III. The Fish Ejected Jonah on Dry Land

"Then Jonah prayed unto the Lord his God out of the fish's belly. . . . And the Lord spake unto the fish, and it vomited out Jonah upon the dry land" (Jonah 2:1, 10).

Jonah in anger ran away from the Lord, his call, and his country. The Lord sent a strong wind and storm after him. Asleep in the ship, he was awakened, taken to task, then by his own request was cast overboard. A great fish, prepared by the Lord, swallowed him. The Lord delivered him from going into the pit, and also provided a ransom for Jonah. This runaway prophet turned to the Lord, prayed, confessed, and vowed he would obey the Lord. When he prayed, the Lord heard his prayer and spoke to the fish, giving it orders to take Jonah to the shore and eject him on the dry land. Then he was discharged from his imprisonment. The fish was prompt in obeying the Lord, and had to be told only once to obey. There was a great change wrought through Jonah's prayer. The prayer of Jonah moved God; then God moved the fish; then the fish moved Jonah; then Jonah moved the Ninevites; then the Ninevites moved God by their repentance and fastings, and this moved God to spare them instead of destroying them.

IV. The Angel Gabriel Brought the Answer to Daniel

"Yea, whiles I was speaking in prayer, even the man Gabriel, whom I had seen in the vision at the beginning, being caused to fly swiftly, touched me about the time of the evening oblation. And he informed me, and talked with me, and said, O Daniel, I am now come forth to give thee skill and understanding" (Dan. 9:21, 22).

Daniel was greatly concerned and burdened for his people, the Jews. He sought to be enlightened concerning their future, their release from captivity, their establishment in Canaan, and the coming of the Messiah in connection with the return of the Jews to their country. Daniel had learned the great lesson of taking everything to the Lord in prayer. While he was engaged in prayer, the Lord sent the answer. Gabriel was sent, and caused to fly swiftly to give skill and understanding to the praying prophet before Daniel was through praying, or had said "Amen." Daniel prayed through before he was through praying. With most people it is the other way, that is, they are through praying before they have prayed through. The answer was given to Daniel while he was praying, while he was on his knees, before he got up, while he had yet more to say to the Lord. The Lord was very ready and willing to hear his prayer and to give him an answer of peace, because Daniel lived in daily righteousness before the Lord. The Lord was greatly pleased with Daniel's desires and devotions.

V. The Fashion of Christ's Countenance Was Altered

"And as He prayed, the fashion of his countenance was altered, and His raiment was white and glistering" (Luke 9:29).

"As He prayed" the glory which had been concealed in Him became revealed. Evidently it was the Deity in Him shining through His humanity. The clause "as He prayed" expresses much, and a great truth in obtaining answers from God. When Christ humbled Himself, He was exalted; and when He abased Himself, He was glorified. The object of His prayer is not stated, but from the context we infer it was concerning His death. It will be as we pray that changes will come to us and to others.

VI. A Passport to Paradise Was Granted to a Thief

"And he said unto Jesus, Lord, remember me when Thou comest into Thy kingdom. And Jesus said unto him, Verily I say unto thee, Today shalt thou be with Me in paradise" (Luke 23:42, 43).

The thief on the cross was highly privileged to be in the presence of the Savior to die. He, a dying sinner, offered his prayer to the dying Savior. It expressed a confession of his lost state, and a faith in Christ as the Savior and King of Israel. He prayed for an entrance into the coming kingdom which was future. What he needed was an immediate answer for immediate salvation to prepare him to enter paradise, even that same day. The Lord knew his immediate need, saved him, and gave him a passport into the glory land. His prayer was the means of his heart being changed and also his destiny. He was changed from a sinner to a saint, from going to hell to go to paradise.

VII. The Place of Assemblage Was Shaken

"And when they had prayed, the place was shaken where they were assembled together, and they were all filled with the Holy Ghost, and they spake the word of God with boldness" (Acts 4:31).

Peter and John were cast into prison overnight by the high priest and the Sadducees; then the next day they were taken to task for boldly preaching Christ. They were also threatened and forbidden to preach in the name of Christ. The believers betook themselves to prayer. There is no law which can keep people from praying. When they were through praying, the Lord gave them a gracious and instant answer. The believers needed a reassurance of God's favor, a manifestation of Christ's presence and help, and a refilling of the Holy Ghost to embolden and empower them to be faithful witnesses of the death and resurrection of Christ. When they prayed, the place was shaken where they were assembled. This was a manifestation of God and His power, and an evidence of the acceptance of their prayers. It helped to establish their faith in the Lord. Being filled with the Holy Ghost (refilled), gave them a greater measure of His fulness and a fresh anointing for new service.

CHAPTER XXI

LOSSES CAUSED FROM A LACK OF PRAYER

The apostle James wrote, "Ye have not, because ye ask not." This text is very simple and easy to understand. The reason many people do not receive answers to prayer is they do not have any prayers to be answered. Probably the greatest lack in most lives is that of prayer. No Christian in this life can fully realize, become conscious of, or fully estimate the dastardly defeats, the disappointing effects, and the great loss of power and opportunities that are caused from a lack of prayer. When we get to heaven, we shall be able to see what God has wrought through the prayers and faith of devout Christians. Many people would not have had any place in the Bible if they had been prayerless and faithless. Men like Moses, Samuel, Elijah, Daniel, and Paul held very prominent places in the Bible, before God, and heaven. Why? They were men of prayer and faith.

I. The Loss of Spiritual Power

Spiritual power comes through prayer and faith and by being in contact with God. Why should God load us down with power, or surcharge us with divine power, when we do not linger in His presence in prayer? There is a reason why spiritual power rests on a Christian or minister. The reason is prayer. There is a reason why church workers are powerless, even a prayerless life. A sad fact in the Christian ministry is to hear of a servant of the Lord who in the past has been prayerful and powerful but now is prayerless and powerless. Some ministers, when they were young and inexperienced, actually experienced more power and success in the ministry because they prayed more than they do now after years of experience.

II. The Loss of Victory

There is always a great danger after a great victory, because many Christian people think the battle is all over and they have reached the top of the hill; therefore, can coast down, or continue on the momentum attained. If they are not on their guard, the danger is they will relax and give up praying. Peter failed to pray when Christ commanded him three times to do so. The result was he lacked the courage and spiritual power in the conflict which so shortly confronted him. He failed when the mob came, and resorted to carnal fighting, employing the sword. He cut one man's ear off, and during the trial of Christ, denied His Lord three times. Because of a lack of prayer, there is no reserve of power laid up; then when the test comes, defeat instead of victory is the result.

III. The Loss of Holy Desires

When the believer fails in his prayer life, he becomes cool and loses his spiritual fervor. The less he prays, the less desire and burden for prayer he possesses. Holy desires come from the Lord. Every holy desire should be cherished and fostered. When the Lord brings a holy desire to any Christian, it is not to tantalize or mock him. Truly, God would have each Christian desire to receive that which He desires to give him. By prayer that desire will grow and faith will realize it. In answer to prayer and faith, God will bring that desire to fruition. The heart needs to be prepared, even as soil, to receive the seed; then when the desire has been planted in the heart, it needs to be guarded and cultivated as a tender plant, which in due time will yield an increase and bear fruit. Christ said, "What things soever ye desire, when ye pray, believe that ye receive them, and ye shall have them." Because of a lack of prayer, the desire begotten within a Christian by the Holy Spirit soon withers and dies. It never matures or comes to fruition.

IV. The Loss of Success

Nothing can be sadder in Christian experience than to live below our privilege, which means many things will forever be left undone. To have been used by the Lord, then to be set aside, or on the shelf, because of a shortcoming in one's prayer life, truly is sad, and, a spiritual tragedy. When we might do good and fail to do so, or fail to accomplish what God would like to do through our prayers, then others will fail to obtain the gospel light or the spiritual help they need, and we become guilty of a spiritual crime.

V. The Loss of Holy Joy

Many people may wonder why they possess so little joy. They need not go far to find the reason. The prayerless Christian is also a joyless Christian. Many, if they were honest, could make this confession. They have little joy because they do not pray much. Their wells of joy have been filled with the many cares of life which have crowded out prayer.

VI. The Loss of Open Doors

Some Christian workers have many open doors. There is always a demand for them. Of course, there is a reason for open doors. God uses them and always has something for them to do because they live in touch with Him through prayer. Others wonder why their service is not sought, or why there seems to be no demand for them. These should make a check on their prayer lives to see if there is a leakage caused from a lack of prayer.

VII. The Loss of a Compassionate Spirit

The people who fail in their prayer lives become self-seeking, near-sighted; are all taken up with themselves; live subjective lives and their souls atrophy. It is then they see the splinters in their brothers' eyes and fail to see the rafters in their own eyes. Another danger is they see the faults in other people while they fail to see their own faults. It is then that they become critical and censorious, condemning others and condoning themselves. A devout saint recently said, "When I am prayed up-to-date, the worst people look good to me, and when I am not prayed up-to-date, the best people look hypocritical to me."

Why should the Lord load the prayerless Christian with spiritual power? Why should He bless the prayerless with crowning victories? Why should the Lord give holy desires and bring them to fruition unto those who come short in their prayer lives? Is there not a reason for barrenness in the lives of God's people? Why do some lack joy and fail to have open doors and there seems to be no demand for them? Is there any way whereby we may discern why some become critical and do not possess a compassionate spirit or carry a soul burden? Is there not a cause? The answer is, Yes; there is a cause. It is the lack of prayer.

CHAPTER XXII

A SPIRIT OF PRAYER

The indwelling of the Holy Spirit is essential to a successful life of prayer. In the past more was heard concerning "a spirit of prayer" than we hear in these present days. The person who does not take time to pray much in secret, who does not take time to be holy, will not be apt to be blessed with a spirit of prayer.

I. Explaining a Spirit of Prayer

Every faithful Christian has regular appointed seasons for prayer. He prays from a sense of duty and of privilege. He prays regardless of his feelings, whether he is disposed or indisposed to pray. This is scriptural, and also pleasing to the Lord. However, to every Christian there comes the call to prayer. Often it is to general prayer, but at times it is to particular or specific prayer. The Christian has many weaknesses. One of them is a weakness in his prayer life. Praying is such a great and noble task that in regard to the manner and often the matter, "we know not what we should pray for as we ought." Prayer, in its possibilities, is so great that we are not capable of doing it the way it deserves to be done. If so great a saint as Paul did not know how to do it the way it should be done, how can we ever do it the way it ought to be done! We cannot do it in ourselves. How good it is to know that "the Spirit maketh intercession for us with groanings which cannot be uttered." A "spirit of prayer" is the Holy Spirit, Who dwells in us and Who helps us, drawing us aside to the secret closet, moving us to pray, inspiring us with a special urge, with earnest desires which are begotten by Him to pour them out to God in prayer. It is then that God is working at this end of the line through the

Spirit. This concern, burden, urge, and drawing aside may give expression in groanings, in tears, and earnest pleadings with God. This is the work of the Holy Spirit, inspiring and blessing us with a "spirit of prayer."

II. Seeking a Spirit of Prayer

The person who is sporadic in his prayer life, is not likely to obtain such a "spirit of prayer," nor will the Holy Spirit be very apt to come to him in special movings to lead him in this manner, for he would not appreciate it or respond to His operations. Before the Christian is fully qualified to seek those special movings of the Spirit, those special seasons of a "spirit of prayer," there needs to be a faithful, daily, intensive, personal, prayer life. The help of the Spirit is to be highly cherished and sought. When the Spirit stirs you up, you should stir yourself up and fall in line. Get into the divine current of prayer. It is well to pray for a "spirit of prayer." If you are barren in your prayer life, confess it and pray for a spiritual rain; pray for a fruitful season; pray for a burden of prayer; pray for a "spirit of prayer"; and pray for the Holy Spirit to come to you and help you in your prayer infirmities.

III. Cherishing a Spirit of Prayer

You should cherish a spirit of prayer. If there is no spirit of prayer in your heart and life, desire it and seek it. Go to the place of prayer and stay in the place of prayer fifteen or thirty minutes, or an hour when it is necessary. Spend enough time on your knees before God until a spirit of prayer comes. God will not disappoint you. He will reward the honest waiting heart; He will tenderize your spirit. Delight in it; cherish it; then let it linger when it comes. When you do not stir yourself when He stirs you, the desired results are not obtained.

IV. Reading What Others Say About Prayer

Prayer is so important we should learn all we can about it, and that from any source. The Bible has much to say about prayer. It should be read with a view of learning more about it and how to become more efficient in praying. Moses was a man of prayer. His prayers should be studied to see how God answered him. Joshua, Samuel, David, Daniel, and Nehemiah were men of prayer. Read what they said about prayer and what is recorded concerning their praying. John the Baptist was a man of prayer. Christ said much about prayer, and taught his disciples the manner and the matter of prayer. There have been men in the past who were highly gifted in praying, and some of these have recorded some lessons they learned about prayer. We may also learn from them. It also is right that every Christian should teach himself to pray and seek all the instruction he can on prayer.

V. Hearing Holy Gifted Men Pray

Probably here is where we receive the best help and the greatest inspiration to pray, that is, hearing gifted men in prayer interceding with God. An example of this fact was when Christ was interrupted by His disciples while He was praying. They were so moved by it that they said, "Lord, teach us to pray as John also taught his disciples." Dr. Kirk has said, "People learn more what prayer is and how to pray in hearing one real prayer than by all the sermons and talks they ever heard or will hear." It is a blessed privilege to be in the presence of holy men who are gifted in praying and hear them plead with God. When a holy saint is in communion with God, weeps, groans, agonizes, and pleads with the Lord, there is a sacred and inspiring influence about it that stirs, grips, and moves the heart of every one who hears and desires to be efficient in praying, such as nothing else will outside of being influenced by the Holy Spirit.

VI. Grieving the Holy Spirit When We Do Not Respond

The Holy Spirit is a Spirit and a Person. He needs a body through which He may work. He works through believers. Of course, He must have the will, the consent, and the co-operation of the believer. When He moves the believer and the believer fails to respond, He is being limited and restricted. When He comes on the believer, moving him with holy desires, holy burdens, and a holy urge to pray, it is then that He desires to do something, and is seeking the employment of the human instrument through whom He may work. When He thus operates on the believer, moving him to pray, it is then that the believer needs to co-operate with the Spirit. When He moves, the believer should move and fall in line. When the Holy Spirit has stirred the believer and the believer has responded to the Spirit, there is operation and co-operation. It is then that the Spirit helps the believer to get a grip on God to move Deity in heaven. However, when the believer is indifferent to the movings of the Spirit and does not respond, the Spirit is grieved; then fervent and effective prayer will not be offered; a great blessing will be lost and there will not be any prayer to be answered. Any one who is guilty of failing to respond when the Spirit has come on him to pray should repent of his great failure and ask to be forgiven, then cherish a spirit of prayer and respond to it always.

VII. Involving Issues in a Spirit of Prayer

Great issues are involved when the Holy Spirit moves a person by a special urge, drawing him aside to pray. If Christians could but realize the issues which are involved when a spirit of prayer comes on them, they would be faithful in the discharge of that duty. God works through human instrumentalities. God the Father in heaven works through Christ, the glorified God-Man, and God the Holy Spirit works on earth through Spirit-filled believers. We are co-workers with God. When the Spirit draws the believer aside for prayer, the issue involved is, God the Father through Christ and God the Holy Spirit through the Christian are seeking to draw together to complete a divine current in which the power and blessing of the Lord may flow. Then it is up to the believer to become the point of contact which completes the circuit. When the divine urge of the Spirit comes on the believer to help him in his infirmities, it is then, as it were, the Lord is saying to him, "For what dost thou make request?" The Christian then should do like Nehemiah did when the king asked him that question. He said, "So I prayed to the God of heaven." Then he asked largely and obtained all he asked. That was an opportune time for Nehemiah. Even so it is with the Christian; when a spirit of prayer comes on him, that will be an opportune time for him to pray. It is then that he may weep, groan, plead, and prevail with God in prayer, and as Jude writes "pray in the Holy Ghost.' All praying in the Holy Ghost is nothing less than the Holy Ghost praying in and through the believer. Let us never allow an opportunity to pass by to pray when the Spirit comes to draw us aside, but allow Him to employ us as the human instrument through whom He may accomplish that great ministry.

CHAPTER XXIII

THE HIGH COST OF PRAYER

In these recent years we have heard much concerning the high cost of living, the high cost of butter, of meat, of clothes, and rent. Little has been said concerning the high cost of prayer. Praying is not a menial task; neither is it a light task. It is costly because it is so valuable. Everything worth-while is costly. The greater the value of an article, the higher will be the cost. The Missionary Tidings relates that a pastor said to the young people in his congregation, "I want you to spend fifteen minutes every day praying for foreign missions. But beware how you pray, for I warn you that it is a very costly experiment." "Costly," they asked in surprise. "Aye, costly," he cried, "It may cost you yourself." The answers to our prayers can not be purchased by money. God's blessings and gifts are free; however, to pray earnestly, efficiently, and effectively is costly.

I. It Will Cost Time

It takes time to pray, sometimes long periods before we have prayed through. It requires time to begin to pray, to get in the spirit of prayer, to get under the burden, to continue in prayer, and to pray through. Time is precious and is God-given. The Bible commands us to redeem it. There can be no better manner of redeeming time than to spend it in prayer. Though it will cost us time, it will be worth every minute we devote to it. When we pray we will accomplish much more than when we do not pray. It will be investing time wisely; it will court the favor and blessing of God; and it will retard the progress of sin and Satan. We will be far ahead by spending much time in prayer. Much time is lost by a lack of prayer.

II. It Will Cost Energy

Intense and fervent praying is such a great task it costs us energy. It is a pouring out of our heart, life, and energy. It will cost mental energy, physical energy, and spiritual energy; however, while there is a giving out of the spiritual, there will be a recharging, which will be greater than the discharging. If fasting is associated with praying, it will expend energy. Again, we repeat, it will be worth it, for there will come to us a spiritual recuperation while the physical energy is expended.

III. It Will Cost Persecutions

Prayer will not go unchallenged by Satan. Persecutions, opposition, and hindrances will come from Satan, worldly people, and even from nominal Christians. There will come inward conflicts, struggles, and onslaughts from the Satanic forces; hatred, opposition, and sneering from sinners; and persecution, ridicule, and misunderstanding from the nominal or non-praying church members. In spite of all these, it will pay to pray.

IV. It Will Cost Humility

Humility is a beautiful and rare virtue. Many people consider it will cost them too much to humble themselves. A person can not be efficient in praying when pride is in the heart. God will not hear a person who has pride in his heart, but He will resist him. In order to pray efficiently and effectively, the offerer must humble himself before God. God has promised to give grace to the humble. God has two arms, a mighty hand (His left hand) which is over us, and His everlasting arm and right hand is underneath us. He will employ the hand we touch. We are commanded to submit ourselves under the mighty hand (left) of God. If we exalt ourselves and come up to that hand, that is the hand which will chasten and bring us down. When we humble ourselves and get low before Him, we will touch

His everlasting arm. This is the arm which will exalt
and bring us up. Humiliation is the way to exaltation
and promotion. Humiliation moves the hand of God to
do for us as we entreat Him. It pays to humble self
before God in prayer.

V. It Will Cost Soul Agony

Prayer is the soul's sincere desire, uttered or unexpressed. All who have prayed earnestly before the
Lord know that they can always pray the best when
their souls are burdened, exercised, and the longing of
the heart has inward agony. This soul agony will lead to
agonizing prayer. When the soul is thus moved to agony,
it moves God. It is then that God will change conditions,
circumstances, and people. Christ in Gethsemane
possessed soul agony. It expressed itself in humility and submission. Men like Martin Luther, Mueller,
John Knox, Brainerd, Whitefield, Finney, Carey and
others possessed soul agony in prayer, which so moved
God that God hearkened to them and gave them their
heart's desire. Such soul burdens were begotten by the
Holy Spirit, and they unburdened themselves before
God in prayer, and He brought to fruition their holy
desires. It pays to possess a soul agony in prayer, for
in the end it will bring great joy to God, to us, and to
others.

VI. It Will Cost Retirement

The person who never desires to get alone with
God does not know much about praying. He who never
seeks to get alone with God, but desires social contact
and to be with other people constantly, does not rise
higher than the people with whom he constantly associates. To become efficient in prayer, there absolutely
must be a desire to be alone with God in prayer that
will lead to retirement and the secret closet to be alone
with God. The most mighty, the most prevailing praying is that which is done in the secret closet. This truth
can be illustrated from the lives of all truly great men
and women of God. Jacob never amounted to much for

God until he spent one night alone with God. David, Elijah, Daniel, and John the Baptist were men who were much alone with God. Whenever they appeared before the public, it could be observed that they had been alone with God. It pays to retire in prayer. The value of retirement in prayer is worth more than the cost.

VII. It Will Cost You Yourself

A person can not be efficient or at his best in prayer that holds himself in reserve, or that is not fully consecrated to the Lord. The person who prays efficiently must be completely yielded to the Lord, and hold himself open and in readiness to be the instrument through whom He may answer that prayer. The Lord said to His disciples, "Pray ye therefore the Lord of the harvest, that He would send forth laborers into His harvest." In just a little while He said, "Behold, I send you forth." By sending them forth, He answered their prayers. When William Carey began to pray for the conversion of the world, it cost him himself, and it cost those who prayed much with him. David Brainerd prayed passionately for the Indians, and it cost him his life after a few years. No person can pray earnestly, fervently, passionately, consistently, and persistently and withhold his labor, time, money, or life. Yes, if you pray thus, it will cost you your labor, your money; and your very life will no longer be yours, but His Who answers your prayers.

Nothing can take the place of prayer. Culture, refinement, ethics, talents, gifts, education, or training can not take the place of prayer. There are no substitutes for prayer and the anointing of the Spirit. The cost of prevailing prayer is great, but it is well worth it. The reward will more than justify the cost.

"O steal away softly to Jesus
  To Him let thy heart be outpoured;
Thy Father which seeth in secret
  Shall give thee a gracious reward."

CHAPTER XXIV

THE SIN OF PRAYERLESSNESS

Prayer is a divine command, a human necessity, and a great privilege; therefore, the neglect of the performance of this duty is sin. It is a sin of omission. The sins of omission are very subtle because they do not bring any alarm or guilt. The sin of prayerlessness is a sin of which we hear very little, and which is not taken to heart or made a concern. Many people should ask God to forgive them because they have come far short in praying; then pray more in order to court the favor of God.

I. It Invokes the Fury of God

"Pour out Thy fury upon the heathen that know Thee not, and upon the families that call not on Thy name" (Jer. 10:25).

No sin provokes God like the sin of idolatry, and no insult comes to God like the insult of ignoring Him. Those who do not pray, do not acknowledge God. Calling on the name of God is something all can do and need to do. God commands it, and man's needs demand it. Since God sends all material and spiritual blessings upon men and men are dependent on His faithfulness, God is grieved when He is ignored. In answer to prayer God saves, blesses, and does things; but when people do not pray, that hinders Him. He pours out His fury on those who are guilty of the sin of prayerlessness.

II. It is a Sin of Omission

"Therefore to him that knoweth to do good, and doeth it not, to him it is sin" (James 4:17).

Praying is doing a good thing. It leads to the doing of many more good things. It is like a good seed which brings forth an increase after its kind. Failing to pray is failing to do good. To abstain from praying will evidently lead to or be the occasion for doing wrong, because of a lack of fortitude, just as truly as praying will keep us from doing wrong and enable us to do right, because it empowers us to do so. The sin of omission is the failure to do good when we know we should do so. The sins of omission are very deceitful because they bring no condemnation, guilt, shame, sorrow, or conviction. They leave no alarm; therefore, many omit and keep on omitting, because they feel that it does no harm; however, it is sin in the sight of God.

III. It Leads to Spiritual Impoverishment
"Ye have not, because ye ask not" (James 4:2)

We might say, "Ye have not answers to prayer, because ye have no prayers to be answered." Prayer, Bible reading, and gospel work feed, strengthen, and build up the inner man. Failing to do so has the opposite effect and leads to spiritual impoverishment. Spiritual impoverishment leads to spiritual defeat. There is no spiritual reserve, joy, or triumph in the life of a prayerless person. When a person is not what he should be, what God wants him to be, and what His grace can make him, it is because of prayerlessness. That person is doing an injustice to himself, to God, and to those around him who need his help. The prayerless person cannot live in spiritual triumph, be a help to other souls, nor can he glorify God.

IV. It Allows Defeat to Come to Others
"And it came to pass, when Moses held up his hand, that Israel prevailed: and when he let down his hand, Amalek prevailed. But Moses' hands were heavy; and they took a stone, and put it under him, and he sat thereon; and Aaron and Hur stayed up his hands, the one on the one side, and the other on the other side; and his hands were steady until the going down of the sun. And Joshua discomfited Amalek and his people with the edge of the sword" (Ex. 17:11-13).

What we do, or fail to do, always involves and effects others. The victory and success of others often are contingent on our prayers. Many people have failed, some have not been converted, and others have gone astray, because some one failed to pray for them. The

above Scripture is a striking illustration of the power
of intercession and the success which may come to
others through our prayers, and, on the other hand, of
the defeat which may come to others because of a lack
of prayer. When Moses interceded, Joshua was victorious; and as soon as he ceased, defeat came to him and
the Amalekites triumphed. When Moses was assisted
by Aaron and Hur who stayed up his hands, Joshua
and his army prevailed. If those who stay at home
would pray for those who have gone forth as ministers
and missionaries, they would be more successful on the
battle front. If those whom God has called to be leaders
and to the front lines do not succeed, many will fail to
be converted and others will be defeated; but much of
the responsibility will rest on those who have failed to
pray for God's leaders.

V. It is a Sin of Neglect

"Moreover as for me, God forbid that I should sin against the
Lord in ceasing to pray for you" (I Sam. 12:23).

The prophet Samuel was a man of great intercession. Through his prayers God brought to pass a revival in Israel, and gave victory over Israel's enemies.
Samuel knew the value of prayer and its possibilities.
He resolved not to be guilty of the sin of neglect by
failing to pray for Israel. He knew that victory and
success were contingent on his prayers. Personal victory and the success of others were dependent on his
praying. He did not become guilty of the sin of neglect
by ceasing to pray for Israel, as is the case of many
people.

VI. It Is Disobedience to God's Commands

"Men ought always to pray, and not to faint" (Luke 18:1).
"I will therefore that men pray every where" (I Tim. 2:8).

All of God's commandments are given for our good.
None can be neglected and men not suffer in doing so.
The command to men to pray is very reasonable, practi-
cal, and profitable for all to obey. The person who prays
will gain by it, and he who does not will be the loser.
The person who prays will reap a twofold blessing,

namely, he has obeyed God and his prayer will be answered. The person who does not pray, will disobey the Lord and also forfeit the blessing of the Lord.

VII. It Leads to Damnation

"For whosoever shall call upon the name of the Lord shall be saved" (Rom. 10:13).

Since those who call on the name of the Lord will be saved, it will be reasonable to assume that all who do not call on the name of the Lord will not be saved. Calling on the name of the Lord is a very simple matter. It is praying to the Lord. There is no distinction made as to race or state, but the condition is that of calling. Those who do not meet this condition will be cut off, lost, and damned. From this, again, we learn that the sin of prayerlessness is great and disastrous.

CHAPTER XXV

THE KNEEOLOGY OF JOSEPH

"And Joseph saw Ephraim's children of the third generation: the children also of Machir the son of Manasseh were brought up upon Joseph's knees" (Gen. 50:23).

We hear much about theology from the pulpit and the class room, but little concerning kneeology. Theology, in its restricted sense, means the doctrine of God. Kneeology means a persistent and consistent life of prayer. Theology is to be believed, and kneeology is to be practiced. Kneeology makes effective theology. Joseph was a man who practiced kneeology. His knees are mentioned several times in his record. Joseph was strong in his knees, that is, in his prayer life.

David said, "I am fearfully and wonderfully made." Man, in his human body, as created by God was made more elaborate, complex, God-like, and with a greater purposeful design than any other living organism. We are particularly interested in how God made the joints between the thighs and the feet called the knees. This enables man to get down low before God in humility so that he may worship his Creator and Redeemer. God intended that man should pray unto Him; therefore, He made him so he could get down on his knees, which in a wonderful way are protected with caps that fit well in standing, walking, sitting, and especially in kneeling. We frequently hear people thanking God for good eyes, for good ears, for good teeth; but why not thank Him for two good knees, then use them for His glory.

I. Joseph on His Knees for Himself

Joseph was a dreamer in his youth and a seer in his old age. We may well believe that Joseph made use of his knees, that is, prayed much in youth, all through life, and in old age. Joseph prayed much for himself.

It is good to pray for self, but our prayers should not stop there. When Joseph went down on his knees in prayer, he came in touch with the everlasting Arm that was underneath him. That Arm brought him up. When Joseph would get down before God, God looked down on him. Joseph was a success wherever he was, and we have reasons to believe he was a man of prayer at home, in Egypt as a slave, in prison, on the throne, and in his own home. Whenever Joseph went down, he always came up. Whenever he was pushed down by anyone, he also went down on his knees; and therefore, always came up and landed on top. Prayer is the secret of a life of success. All great men and women of God who have blessed the world are an illustration of this fact; they prayed much.

II. Joseph on His Knees for Others

Joseph blessed every one who came in touch with him. He was a comfort and blessing to his father. He was a blessing to his brethren, though they knew it not. They returned evil for good, and hated him without a cause. Joseph was a blessing to Potiphar's house. Whatsoever he did the Lord made it to prosper. Potiphar was highly favored in having Joseph in his home. In prison he was made a blessing to all the prisoners. He brought cheer and blessing into the prison. Joseph was made a blessing to Pharaoh and the whole land of Egypt. In a time of crisis, he was a blessing to a famishing world. The secret for all this was, Joseph prayed for his father, his brethren, for Potiphar, for all the prisoners, for Pharaoh, and for the land of Egypt.

III. Joseph on His Knees for His People

Joseph's dreams were long in being fulfilled. He prayed, waited, and hoped for many years. The years he spent in prison were not in vain nor spent idly. If we could but know it, he prayed in prison, prayed persistently, prayed more, and prayed on. During these years he did not forget his father and his brethren. We have reasons to believe that he became very homesick,

being separated from his father for twenty-two years.
Thirteen of these years were spent as a slave and in
prison. In the fourteenth year of his separation, he was
promoted, and became second ruler on the throne of
Egypt. Pharaoh gave him a wife and a home of his own.
During the seven years of plenty and prosperity, two
sons were born unto him. The first one he named Manasseh. The English for this name means "Forgetting." His
own words were, "God hath made me to forget all my
toil and my father's house." He no longer was homesick, but contented and happy. However, his prayers did
not cease for his own, but he continued to pray for
them during the seven years of plenty and the years
of famine. We may well believe that he also prayed to
God how he should deal with his brethren when they
would come to Egypt for food. He was confident that
the famine would bring them into Egypt. We are made
to marvel at the manner in which he dealt with them
when they came. Surely he was divinely inspired in
his method of dealing with them. After the reconciliation of his brethren, he undoubtedly continued to pray
for his own people all through his life.

IV. Joseph on His Knees for His Own Children

Children are a godly heritage from the Lord. It is
a solemn responsibility to bring children into the world.
God will hold parents responsible for their children. It
is their privilege to first lead their children to the Lord.
They need to be brought up around the family altar. If
children are going to be brought up right, the parents
must go down on their knees in prayer for them.

Joseph had two sons, Manasseh and Ephraim. Joseph
was much on his knees for Manasseh and Ephraim.
His descendants increased during his lifetime. We read
"Joseph saw Ephraim's children of the third generation." He became a great, great grandfather. Joseph as
a father prayed for his children; as a grandfather he
prayed for his grandchildren; as a great grandfather he
prayed for his great grandchildren; and as a great, great
grandfather he prayed for his great, great grand-

children. What a father was he! What a heritage he left to his descendants! What a blessing he became! What good resulted from his prayers! No wonder his descendants were brought up well, for he went down on his knees in prayer to God for his children.

V. Joseph's Knees Were a Place for Instruction

All children are interested in good stories, and like to hear the experiences of those who are older. Children like to sit on their father's knees while he tells them something interesting. While the children are young is the time to mold their lives. Good stories and good instructions have a powerful influence in molding young lives for good and for God.

Four generations were brought up on Joseph's knees. He had many interesting experiences to tell them of his youth, his trials, and his victories. The years of plenty and of famine in Egypt left their impress and became sacred history. No one could better tell this history than Joseph. How delighted his descendants were to hear him tell it! Then think how interestingly he could tell it!

No sooner did one generation grow up and become too old to receive instruction from Joseph's knees, than another generation was ready to be brought up on his knees. Parents, take your children on your knees, and teach them the right way by telling them good Bible stories.

VI. Joseph's Knees Were a Place for Correction

The knees are not only a good place for instruction, but they also are a good place for correction. Parents should use their knees more in bringing up their children. That is, they should go down on their knees in prayer that their children may be brought up right; then take them on their knees to instruct them in the ways of righteousness. If this does not bring the desired results, and the children are unruly, they need to be brought up on the knees and disciplined, or to be a little plainer, corrected, and chastened. This is not pleasant, but the results will be good. Some parents may say they love their children too much to punish them. This is not love, but human weakness. Proverbs is a book for the young. There we read: "He that spareth the rod hateth his son: but he that loveth him chasteneth him betimes" (Prov. 13:24). And, "Withhold not correction from the child: for if thou beatest him with the rod, he shall not die . . . and shall deliver his soul from hell" (Prov. 23:13, 14). Again, "Correct thy son, and he shall give thee rest; yea, he shall give delight unto thy soul" (Prov. 29:17). Correction should be given in love.

VII. Joseph's Knees—A Place Where His Children Kneeled

Praying for our children is good; taking them on our knees to instruct them is good; taking them on our knees for correction is good, but this is not going far enough. There is one more step to be taken. They need to be made to kneel down on their own knees at our knees and instructed to pray for themselves. What can be more interesting and beautiful than a child kneeling by its parent's knees, and there in prayer call on the name of the Lord. Many have been saved there. Let us practice kneeology. The results will be blessed. Like Joseph, our own souls will be enriched by the blessing of the Lord, and the lives of others will be benefited.

CHAPTER XXVI

GOD HEARKENS TO MEN

God has given many commandments in His Word to men. But where are the men who will obey and believe them? One of the most inspiring, heart-gripping, and stirring facts of the Bible and Christian experience is that of men who did as God commanded them, then entreated God, Who hearkened to them. One of the saddest, most pathetic, and calamitous things that can happen to any individual is to get in a state in which God will not listen to his cries. The conduct of king Saul led on until God would not speak to him nor listen to his voice. He could not hear from God by prophet, priest, or sacrifice. In the days of his defeat and death, he sought the help of a witch. The sun set in his life behind storm clouds. Great delight comes to a Christian in doing God's will and in receiving answers to prayer. Seven Bible examples are given of men who did as the Lord commanded them. They entreated the Lord and He hearkened to them.

I. Jacob Demanded a Divine Blessing

"And he said, I will not let Thee go, except Thou bless me. ... And He blessed him there" (Gen. 32:26, 29).

Jacob was brought under the mighty hand of God Who laid hold of him, then God prevailed with him. God gained the desired object of Jacob. Jacob then laid hold on the Lord, and said, "I will not let Thee go, except Thou bless me." Jacob gained the desired object from the Lord. The Lord made a prince of God out of Jacob. God first prevailed with Jacob; then Jacob prevailed with God. Jacob entreated the Lord and He hearkened unto him and blessed him before He departed. Because God first prevailed with Jacob, it was possible for Jacob to prevail with God. It is impossible to prevail with God until God has first prevailed with us. It also is impossible to prevail with men until we first have prevailed with God. Jacob was blessed so much by the Lord that he could bless others. When he said, "Bless me," he besought God and demanded a blessing which would help him to rise above every opposing element. Jacob had so much of the blessing and power of God about him that Esau and four hundred armed men were overpowered. Jacob blessed Pharaoh twice, and he blessed his sons before he died.

II. Moses Entreated God and He Hearkened

"And the Lord said unto Moses . . . let Me alone . . . and Moses besought the Lord his God, and said, Lord, why doth Thy wrath wax hot against Thy people . . . remember Abraham, Isaac, and Israel, thy servants. . . . And the Lord repented of the evil which He thought to do unto His people" (Exodus 32:9-14).

Of Moses, more than of any other man in the Bible, it is recorded, "he did as the Lord commanded." On the other hand, the Lord hearkened to Moses more than He did to any other man. We may readily see the reason why the Lord hearkened to Moses. It was because Moses did as the Lord commanded. The Lord and Moses were so intimate that they conversed face to face in an audible voice. The Lord hearkened to Moses in Egypt, at the Red Sea, and at Mount Sinai. When the golden calf was made and God was insulted, Moses would not allow God to destroy the entire nation, but reasoned with the Lord, and the Lord gave heed to him. In the above Scripture the Lord said to Moses, "Let Me alone." (Deity crying out unto humanity.) Moses had so much power with God that he implored the Lord and He readily hearkened unto him. This reveals the power a man has with God who fully obeys Him. God trusts those who fully trust and obey Him.

III. Joshua Commanded the Sun and Moon to Stand Still

"Then spake Joshua to the Lord in the day when the Lord delivered up the Amorites, . . . and he said in the sight of Israel,

Sun, stand thou still upon Gibeon; and thou, Moon, in the valley of Ajalon. And the sun stood still, and the moon stayed, until the people had avenged themselves upon their enemies" (Joshua 10:12, 13).

Joshua was God's leader for Israel. He was doing what the Lord called him to do; that was destroying the Canaanites. In his battle against the five kings that had confederated to destroy Israel, Joshua had received encouragement from the Lord. He, with the army of Israel, marched one night twenty-six miles and fought all day against the Amorites. Joshua saw that the battle was going to be long and hard and that unless he had more time he could not finish it by the time the sun set. The sun was overhead and the moon was about to set. Joshua needed more time; therefore, in the name and power of the Lord he said, "Sun, stand still upon Gibeon; and thou, Moon, in the valley of Ajalon." God answered instantly, and the sun stood still and the moon stayed. As we consider the account of the miracle, we can not help but be impressed tremendously with the fact that God heard and answered the cry of a man, and held up the universe to give him time to finish the battle.

IV. Samson Desired Supernatural Strength

"And Samson called unto the Lord, and said, O Lord God, remember me, I pray Thee, and strengthen me, I pray Thee, only this once, O God, that I may be at once avenged of the Philistines for my two eyes" (Judge 16:28).

Samson was divinely called and endued to begin to deliver Israel from the Philistines. God called him to be a Nazarite. No razor was to come on his head. As long as he conducted himself properly, controlled himself, and kept his Nazarite vow, the Spirit and power of the Lord rested on him. It seems he possessed a greater gift than he did grace. He could have had sufficient grace to outbalance his gifts had he been faithful to the Lord and not fellowshiped the Philistines. After he gave away the secret of his strength, the Philistines shaved his head and goughed out his eyes. He was placed in prison where he was compelled to grind the grain for his enemies. Evidently he repented a thousand times for his folly. Day by day his repentance grew, and so did his hair. When his hair was long, he was called on to make sport for the Philistines on one of the feast days in the temple of their god Dagon. Samson offered an earnest, intense prayer, as that of a dying man. He prayed for superhuman strength. He recognized his strength as coming from the Lord. He did not count his life dear to himself, but was willing to sacrifice his life in order that he might finish his course. The Lord gave him strength to do it. His purpose was inspired by a holy zeal and for the glory of God. So earnest and intense was his prayer that God hearkened to him and clothed him with the power of the Almighty. Though he died with the Philistines, he did not die as one of them, but as a hero of faith.

V. Elisha Requested God to Smite an Army with Blindness

"And Elisha prayed, and said, Lord, I pray Thee, open his eyes, that he may see. And the Lord opened the eyes of the young man; and he saw: and, behold, the mountain was full of horses and chariots of fire round about Elisha. . . . Elisha prayed unto the Lord, and said, Smite this people, I pray Thee, with blindness. And He smote them with blindness according to the word of Elisha" (II Kings 6:17, 18).

Elisha was designated as "the man of God." He was obedient to his prophetic office, and was God's man in God's will. By doing what the Lord wanted him to do, the Lord did what Elisha asked Him to do. In answer to Elisha's petition, the Lord instantly hearkened to him and opened the eyes of his servant that he saw the unseen things, even an army of horses and chariots from heaven that filled the mountain around them. As Elisha prayed again, "Lord, Smite this army with blindness," the Lord did as Elisha entreated Him. After Elisha led this army into Samaria, he again petitioned the Lord by saying, "Lord, open the eyes of these men, that they may see," and the Lord did instantly as Elisha implored Him.

VI. Peter, in the Name of the Lord Commanded a Lame Man to Walk

"Then Peter said, Silver and gold have I none; but such as I have give I thee: In the name of Jesus Christ of Nazareth rise up and walk" (Acts 3:6).

Simon Peter was a unique character. He followed the Lord, but sometimes made blunders. The Lord fully restored him and commanded him to feed His lambs and sheep. The Lord also assured him that His divine hand would gird him. Then the Lord informed him that He would give him the keys of the kingdom of heaven, and whatsoever he would bind on earth would be bound in heaven, and whatever he loosed on earth would be loosed in heaven. This refers to the power of prayer and the power of the words of a man of God when they are uttered in the name of Christ. Peter became a man of prayer. When he and John went to the house of prayer at the hour of prayer, they met a lame man asking for alms at the gate. Peter said, "Silver and gold have I none," however, as a man of God and prayer he had wealth in poverty, and he had power with God and men. Silver and gold can do much, but prayer can do more. Money is not omnipotent, but prayer moves an omnipotent God. Peter said, "In the name of Jesus Christ of Nazareth rise up and walk." The Lord hearkened to Peter's command and immediately healed the lame man.

VII. Paul, in the Name of the Lord Commanded a Demon to Depart

"But Paul, being grieved, turned and said to the spirit, I command thee in the name of Jesus Christ to come out of her. And he came out the same hour" (Acts 16:18).

Paul was a man of prayer, and he too had power with God and men. He was divinely led to go into Europe to preach the gospel. Satan bitterly opposed the gospel being taken to a new continent. The first great event in the new continent was the conversion of Lydia and her household. The next great event was the casting out of a demon. The demon in the girl spoke the truth, but it came from an unclean source. Satan confessing Christ is more subtle than denying Christ, for he confesses to oppose. Christ did not allow demons to confess Him, but silenced them. Paul lived in touch with the Lord, which enabled him to employ the name of Christ, and in the name of Christ he commanded the demon to depart, and immediately the demon came out. This girl immediately lost her satanic gift of fortune telling.

Some years ago an aged minister related that when he was a young preacher preaching at an eastern Camp Meeting, an old black woman behind him on the platform would shout, then come down with her foot, and say, "O Lord, bless that boy preacher." The preacher said he felt a divine current that charged him with divine power go through him from his head to the feet. After a while she again prayed, "O Lord, bless that boy preacher." Again a divine current went through him. The blessing of the Lord was so great he did not know whether he could endure it. Again she prayed, "O Lord, bless that boy preacher," and again greater blessings fell on him. The preacher thought if he lived through to the end of that sermon, he would enquire who this black lady was who could so command God that He would instantly answer as by an electric current. When he was through and gave the altar call, scores came running to the altar as seekers. About forty other preachers and workers were exhorting and pleading with people to seek the Lord. He was not concerned so much about the other preachers and people, or the seekers at the altar; but he wanted to know who this black woman was who could command God that He would answer instantly. He went up on the platform to this aged black woman, and found out it was none other than dear old black Amanda Smith. To live in touch and tune with God, to be able to entreat Him so that He will hearken to us, is worth more than silver or gold, honor or fame. This power and right will be given to us only as we obey His commandments, then linger much with God in the secret closet and prevail with Him.

CHAPTER XXVII

LOCKING AND UNLOCKING POWER OF PRAYER

It has been said that prayer is the key which unlocks heaven's door. A key is an instrument to move the bolt of a lock. The term "key" also is employed as that which serves to solve or explain some problem, condition, or situation. Of course, the right key needs to be employed for the right lock. Heaven is spoken of as having windows and doors or gates. Prayer, prevailing prayer, coupled with faith is the right key to open heaven's door, which will release the blessings of God. Many things come to pass only as we pray, and many things have not come to pass because of a lack of prayer. Prayer and faith form a key which always fits heaven's door and also every problem, condition, or situation.

I. By Prayer Moses Unlocked the Red Sea

"And the Lord said unto Moses, Wherefore criest thou unto Me? speak unto the children of Israel, that they go forward: but lift thou up thy rod, and stretch out thine hand over the sea, and divide it: and the children of Israel shall go on dry ground through the midst of the sea" (Ex. 14:15, 16).

The Lord and Moses led Israel out of Egypt through the wilderness by the way of the Red Sea. Here the people were hemmed in a place where there were craggy rocks and hills on one side, the sea before them, and Pharaoh and his army blocked the way behind them, getting ready to pounce on them. Humanly speaking there was no way out, or of escape. Moses cried to the Lord. He employed the key of prayer and it unlocked that critical situation. God was moved and He made a road through the midst of the Sea, which allowed the children of Israel to pass through on dry ground. There come times in the lives of God's people in which He leads them into tight places where the only way out is to employ the key of prayer, which will unlock the place to allow them to pass out and on the way.

II. By Prayer Elijah Locked the Heavens

Elias was a man subject to like passions as we are, and he prayed earnestly that it might not rain: and it rained not on the earth by the space of three years and six months" (James 5:17).

Ahab and Israel had insulted God by going into idolatry. This provoked God and forfeited His blessings. Elijah was the Lord's prophet who was sent to Ahab with the startling message, "there shall not be dew nor rain these years, but according to my word." Elijah employed the key of prayer, and so tightly did he lock the heavens that for the space of three years and six months not one drop of rain or dew fell. This enraged Ahab so that he sought for Elijah throughout the entire earth during the period the heavens were locked; however, God hid Elijah and took care of him.

III. By Prayer Elijah Unlocked the Heavens

"And he prayed again, and the heavens gave rain, and the earth brought forth her fruit" (James 5:18).

The day came when Elijah appeared again unto Ahab, and the issue had to be settled as to who was the true and living God. The test was made, and the God of Abraham, of Isaac and Jacob, answered by fire. The people had to acknowledge Him, for the Baal worshipers failed in the test. Now the time had come for the heavens to be opened and for rain to come. Elijah employed the same key to open the heavens which he had employed to lock them. This time it became necessary for him to pray seven times before there was an evidence of rain. Here is an encouraging Scripture that should encourage us to employ the key of prayer. Elijah was a man subject to like passions as we are. Consider what many people could do if they would pray earnestly!

IV. By Prayer Daniel Unlocked Secrets

"Then Daniel went to his house, and made the thing known

to Hananiah, Mishael, and Azariah, his companions: that they would desire mercies of the God of heaven concerning this secret; that Daniel and his fellows should not perish with the rest of the wise men of Babylon. Then was the secret revealed unto Daniel in a night vision. Then Daniel blessed the God of heaven" (Dan. 2:17-19).

Daniel was another character who was skilful in employing the key which locks and unlocks critical situations. Daniel and his three companions had not been consulted to make known to the king the dream which he had forgotten, yet they were sought first to be executed. He requested that some time be given him, and he assured the executioners that he would give the king a satisfactory answer. Daniel and his three companions employed the key which unlocks secrets; and the God Whom they served and trusted, and Who had given Nebuchadnezzar a dream in his sleep, but also had taken it away from him during his sleep leaving him with a troubled mind, gave the answer to Daniel in his sleep, who then gave it to Nebuchadnezzar. Daniel was very careful to give God all the glory for unlocking the secret of the future to him.

V. By Prayer Daniel Locked the Lions' Mouths

"Now when Daniel knew that the writing was signed, he went into his house; and his windows being open in his chamber toward Jerusalem, he kneeled upon his knees three times a day, and prayed, and gave thanks before his God, as he did aforetime" (Dan. 6:10).

"My God hath sent His angel, and hath shut the lions' mouths, that they have not hurt me: forasmuch as before Him innocency was found in me; and also before thee, O king, have I done no hurt" (Dan. 6:22).

Daniel was a man of prayer. The greatest concern in his life was to pray to his God. This he did daily three times; therefore, he was skilful in the employment of the key which unlocked secrets. Because he prayed three times daily after a law had been made that no one was to ask any petition of any one except the king for thirty days, he was cast into the den of lions to become food for them. He did not fear his enemies nor the lions. Because he was faithful in his prayer life (and no doubt he prayed for his preservation), God shut the lions' mouths. He locked their jaws so that they had a certain type of "lockjaw." It is unscriptural to picture Daniel in the den with the lions' mouths open ready to devour him. With Daniel the "prayer key" was just as effective in locking the lions' mouths as it was in unlocking secrets. Daniel did not need to pray much at the time he was cast into the den for his prayers in the past availed for him at the present. He was right, and did not have to get right; therefore, his prayers availed for him. Some people, in time of emergency, must get right before their prayers will go through. Those who have kept right can pray in an emergency and their prayers will go through immediately. The prayer of a righteous person will avail much more than the prayer of a person who must first get right.

VI. By Prayer the Early Church Unlocked the Prison

"Peter therefore was kept in prison: but prayer was made without ceasing of the church unto God for him . . . and, behold, the angel of the Lord came upon him, . . . and the angel said unto him, Gird thyself, and bind on thy sandals. And so he did. And he saith unto him, Cast thy garment about thee, and follow me . . . when they were past the first and the second ward, they came unto the iron gate that leadeth unto the city; which opened to them of his own accord: and they went out" (Acts 12:5-10).

Herod had killed James with the sword. This pleased the Jews so well that he apprehended Peter and cast him into prison, intending to kill him after the feast of the Jews. The Bible says, "But prayer was made without ceasing of the church unto God for him." The night before the day which had been set for his execution, God, in answer to prayer, sent an angel to deliver him. The chains miraculously dropped off, and the inner and outer gates opened of their own accord. Peter did not unlock the gates and the angel did not break them open, "But prayer of the church" explains it all. Peter and the soldiers were asleep, but God and the saints were awake. Prayer in this case was stronger than a king, a prison, chains, soldiers, gates, locks, sin, and Satan. We can pray people out of trouble.

VII. By Prayer Paul and Silas Unlocked the Prison Stocks

"And at midnight Paul and Silas prayed, and sang praises unto God: and the prisoners heard them. And suddenly there was a great earthquake, so that the foundations of the prison were shaken: and immediately all the doors were opened, and every one's bands were loosed" (Acts 16:25, 26).

Satan tried to prevent the gospel from taking hold in Europe. He occasioned the imprisonment of Paul and Silas. Their bodies were bruised and their feet made fast in stocks. These two evangelists could not sleep, neither could they preach, but they could and did pray. It was midnight when they prayed. Their God, Who does not sleep, heard them. Midnight is just as good a time to pray as midday. The subject of their prayers is not stated. We can only conjecture that they prayed for their enemies, for success, guidance, preservation, divine favor, and for deliverance. While these two were praying, a third One was present, for He said, "Where two or three are gathered together in My name, there am I in the midst." They were locked in prison and locked in stocks, but they employed the key which unlocks difficult situations. God heard their praises and prayers and sent an earthquake that shook the prison which released Paul and Silas. A revival followed in the prison, and these preachers were set free.

CHAPTER XXVIII

ESSENTIAL ELEMENTS IN EFFECTIVE PRAYING

Every Christian should seek to become efficient in prayer. There are seven elements which will be considered as entering into effective praying. When these laws are observed and their conditions met, they will lead to successful praying. The Christian should grow in his praying ability, even as he grows in the Christian graces. This will lead to a holy and useful life.

I. Obedience to God's Commandments

"And whatsoever we ask, we receive of Him, because we keep His commandments, and do those things that are pleasing in His sight" (I John 3:22).

This commandment is very plain and positive. It requires little explanation and may be practiced very easily. The answers to our prayers and growth in the Christian life are contingent on our obedience to God. A consistent and persistent prayer life will have a great bearing on our victory, joy, and usefulness. God can not be prevailed on as long as His commandments are not obeyed, but He very gladly will give whatsoever we ask because we keep His commandments. The conditions are very simple and they may be complied with very easily, even asking, keeping His commandments, and doing those things which are pleasing in His sight.

II. Submission to God's Will

"And He was withdrawn from them about a stone's cast, and kneeled down, and prayed, saying, Father, if Thou be willing, remove this cup from Me: nevertheless not My will, but Thine, be done" (Luke 22:41, 42).

"And this is the confidence that we have in Him, that if we ask any thing according to His will, He heareth us" (I John 5:14).

No man can force God to do that which is against

His will. We must let Him decide for us and plan our lives. When the will conforms to His will, He will let us have our will. If we want what God wants us to have, we can have what we want. God is not hard to please when we want to please Him; neither is He hard to get along with if we want to get along with Him. One of the greatest missions in life is submission to God's will. We absolutely can not wish for anything better than His will for us. We should seek His will in all things, then conform to His will, for that will be the way to get our prayers answered. If we know that anything is not according to His will for us, we should not pray for that thing. When we pray in His will, that will increase our faith and eliminate doubts. We should be careful not to say too often in our prayers "if it be Thy will," for that may imply doubt, and leave a loophole to get out of the conflict and console ourselves without any answer. It is then that some people may say, "Well, I guess it was not His will to answer our prayers." Fervent prayer incites conflict and demands faith and courage. There are some things we positively know are His will, such as the salvation of sinners and those things He has promised in His Word. When we know a thing is God's will, we should ask Him for it with courage and faith.

III. Humility of Character

"If My people, which are called by My name, shall humble themselves, and pray, and seek My face, and turn from their wicked ways; then will I hear from heaven, and will forgive their sin, and will heal their land" (II Chron. 7:14).

Humility is freedom from pride and arrogance, a right estimate of self as being unworthy of God's favors, a feeling of lowliness. Humility is a characteristic of the Christian. It should never be regarded as baseness. Humility of heart is an element which greatly moves God. Nothing brings as much promotion and exaltation from God as humility. This is the one element which brings God down to us and moves Him to place His arm underneath us and lift us up. James wrote, "Humble yourselves in the sight of the Lord.

and He shall lift you up." Peter wrote, "Humble yourselves therefore under the mighty hand of God, that He may exalt you in due time." Humility not only brings promotion, but it also is an element that moves God to do as we ask Him in our prayers.

Some years ago The London Times told the story of a petition that was being circulated for signatures. It was a time of great excitement, and this petition was intended to have a great influence in the House of Lords, but there was one word left out of the petition. Instead of reading "We humbly beseech thee," it simply read "We beseech thee." Because the word "humbly" was left out of the petition, it was ruled out. If we want to make an appeal to God in heaven, we must humble ourselves before Him and with humility of heart and life make our petition known; then He will not rule the prayer out, neither leave us disappointed.

IV. Holiness of Heart and Life

"I will therefore that men pray everywhere, lifting up holy hands, without wrath and doubting" (I Tim. 2:8).

Holiness is God-likeness. It is a moral attribute of God which involves the will. God wills to be holy, and He is greatly pleased with all who will to be holy. Holiness makes heaven a possibility. We are commanded to follow after holiness. Holiness should be sought after as an experience and as a practice. Holiness is begun in regeneration, continued in sanctification, and consummated in glorification. When holiness is followed, God is greatly pleased. If we want our prayers answered, we must follow after holiness.

V. Fervency of Spirit

"The effectual fervent prayer of a righteous man availeth much" (James 5:16).

Bishop Hall wrote, 'It is not the arithmetic of our prayers, how many there are; nor the rhetoric of our prayers, how eloquent they be, nor the geometry of our prayers, how long they be; nor the music of our prayers, how sweet our voice may be; nor the logic of our prayers, how argumentative they may be; nor the method of our prayers, how orderly they may be; nor the divinity of our prayers, how good the doctrine may be—which God cares for. He looks not for the horny knees which St. James is said to have had through the assiduity of prayer; we might be like St. Bartholomew, who is said to have had a hundred prayers for the morning, and as many for the evening, and all might be of no avail. Fervency of spirit is that which availeth much. 'The effectual fervent prayer of a righteous man availeth much.'" The effectual prayer is an energetic prayer, a prayer that is inwrought, inbreathed by the Spirit. Fervent means to boil, to be hot. James Montgomery who wrote a song on prayer expresses this thought in these words,

"The motion of a hidden fire
That trembles in the heart."

This fervor needs to be both human and divine. The prayer which "availeth much" must be a double prayer. Not merely the glow and fervor of the person praying, nor the fervor of the Holy Spirit alone, but the one in the other is what makes the prayer fervent, as well as effectual. The warmth of the human heart needs to be set ablaze by the fire of the Holy Spirit. Such a prayer will go through to the throne of grace, for it is a prayer in a prayer. James gives an example of this fact when he said, "Elijah was a man subject to like passions as we are, and he prayed earnestly (in his prayer, margin)" or "he prayed in his prayer." The prayer in a prayer is the power that carries the petition to God, and nothing can hinder it from going through.

VI. Regularity in Prayer

"Evening, and morning, and at noon, will I pray, and cry aloud: and He shall hear my voice" (Ps. 55:17).

"Now when Daniel knew that the writing was signed, he went into his house; and his windows being open in his chamber toward Jerusalem, he kneeled upon his knees three times a day, and prayed, and gave thanks before his God, as he did aforetime" (Dan. 6:10).

Surely the regularity of our prayer life is taken into consideration by God when we pray. The person who is irregular or spasmodic in his prayer life, and prays only occasionally or when he has come to an emergency, then prays only to get over the crisis and then again fails to pray until another need arises, does not need to expect answers to his prayers. Such a person is not giving God a square deal in his prayer life. God is pleased with our daily, that is, our regular prayer life and with our objective motives. This will prevail on Him to answer our prayers.

VII. Faith in God and His Promises

"And all things, whatsoever ye shall ask in prayer, believing, ye shall receive" (Matt. 21:22).

We honor God by believing in His goodness, greatness, and beneficence. We cannot honor or please God in any greater way than that of believing what He has said, then ask and live like we believe. It is written that Alexander the Great had a famous philosopher in his court. He became straitened in his circumstances, and came to the great conqueror for help, who said that his request should be granted and he receive out of his treasury whatever he wanted. He demanded immediately in his sovereign's name ten thousand pounds. The treasurer became surprised at the demand of so large a sum, declined to pay it, came to the conqueror, and remonstrated. Alexander the Great listened; then said, "Let the money be paid instantly. I am delighted with this philosopher's way of thinking; he has done me a singular honor; by the largeness of his request he shows me the high idea he has conceived both of my superior wealth and my royal munificence." Faith in God pleases Him and moves Him to answer prayer.

CHAPTER XXIX

PRAYING FOR MATERIAL THINGS

Prayer is a privilege. It is our privilege to take everything to God in prayer. We often sing that good song:

"What a Friend we have in Jesus,
All our sins and griefs to bear!
What a privilege to carry
Everything to God in prayer!
Oh, what peace we often forfeit,
Oh, what needless pain we bear,
All because we do not carry
Everything to God in prayer."

We should thank God for the privilege of taking everything to Him in prayer, then practice it in our every day life. Some people may be possessed with the thought that we should not pray about everything, nor trouble the Lord with our material and every day affairs, but only pray about spiritual and eternal matters. Some reason that the common and daily matters in our lives do not concern God. From the very fact that we are His children and He is our Father and concerned about us, our concerns become His concerns. What concerns God should concern us, and what concerns us surely concerns Him. The great and the little things may all be taken to God in prayer. It is stated that Hudson Taylor prayed that the fast-closed doors of China might be opened, and they were opened. On another occasion he prayed for a lost but needed pin, and he found it.

After we have been saved, it is our privilege to pray about the great spiritual objectives; however, the Lord is also pleased for us to pray for our material, physical, and personal needs. If a thing is right for us to desire and right for us to have, it is right for us to ask the Lord for it. Whatever we do, or desire to have, we should ask the blessing of the Lord upon it; and if we cannot ask the blessing of the Lord upon it, we should not do it, or ask the Lord for it.

I. Praying for Food

God is interested in our food and eating. Christ taught us to pray after this manner, ". . . Give us this day our daily bread." In Eden, God made a gracious provision for Adam and Eve by making many trees with fruit on them for their sustenance. After the fall, man was commanded to work and sweat to provide for his living. The help of the Lord is needed in raising any crop. It is He Who gives the increase. It was the Lord Who sent Joseph into Egypt to lay up food in days of prosperity against the days of famine. The Lord sent manna from heaven to Israel during the forty years of their wanderings. The Lord provided for His servant Elijah, first by using the ravens to bring food to him; then later the Lord arranged for a widow to sustain him; then after that an angel fed him two times while he was lying under a juniper tree. On one occasion Christ fed five thousand men, and on another occasion He fed four thousand. Two times Christ enabled His disciples to catch their nets full of fishes. The Lord knows that we are dependent upon food for our physical sustenance. It is proper and good to pray the blessing of the Lord upon our planting, and to trust Him for a bountiful increase. Many of God's children could testify that God in answer to their prayers has given them bumper crops. Many saints throughout the entire age have prayed for food, and God in a gracious manner has answered their prayers in providing for their physical needs. If all the answers to prayer for food could be grouped together, there would be multitudes of them, and many interesting stories could be written on how God provided for His own.

II. Praying for Clothes

The Lord is not only concerned about our food, but also about the clothes that we wear. God is concerned about our appearance, our comfort, and our modesty. Originally, God clothed man with righteousness, holiness, and glory. Sin stripped man in the fall of his glory and honor. The Lord God clothed Adam and Eve with the skins of some slain animals. The Israelites wandered in the wilderness for forty years and were sustained by the Lord Who made their shoes and clothes to wear during this entire period. Their garments did not become threadbare, nor did their shoes wear out. Their shoes and clothes were just as good when they entered Canaan as when they came out of Egypt. Many saints have been poor in material things and were dependent upon God for their clothes. Multitudes could testify how God through some one else sent them shoes or clothes, which were the right size, that came in answer to prayer. Others could testify that God in answer to prayer blessed their clothes and caused them to wear much longer than clothes ordinarily wear. It is the privilege of every child of God when in need of clothes to take it to the Lord in prayer.

III. Praying for a House

The Lord is not only concerned about our food and clothes, but also a place for us to live. Certainly God is concerned that men shall have shelter from rain, cold, and the elements, and a decent, comfortable place in which to live. Often God's children are poor in material things but rich in faith. When any are in need of a house or a new place of residence, it is their privilege to take it to the Lord in prayer. Here again, many saints could testify how graciously God has answered prayer for them in giving them a house, or in helping them to find the right house in the right community,or making it possible for them to purchase a house; while others could tell how the Lord enabled them to sell their houses at the right time when they changed location. The Lord knows how to shift people about to make room for His own, or where there is a house for rent or sale. The Lord is a good real estate agent. It is right for God's children to take to the Lord in prayer their need for a house in which to live.

IV. Praying for Money

Money has its place and value. It has proven a blessing and help to some, but a curse and hindrance to others. Money is not sinful in itself. It is the "love of money" that becomes the root of all evil, and it is the misuse of a good thing that becomes sin. Consecrated money is a blessing and needful for the Christian and the cause of Christ. The Christian gets in need of many things such as food, clothes, rent money, carfare, and all things that are essential to living. Money is a medium of exchange. Financial distress has been the condition of many Christians. Whenever the Christian is in need of money, it is his privilege to take it to the Lord in prayer. Interesting and thrilling answers to prayer could be related by a large per cent of Christians, how God answered prayer in providing for their temporal needs, in sending money to them in the nick of time. These have been blessed and joyfully surprised, not merely in that God answered prayer, but in the manner He answered and by the different sources through which it came to them.

V. Praying for Protection

The saint of God is hated by Satan and wicked men. His life is beset by many dangers, seen and unseen. Moreover, we are living in a dangerous world. There are dangers in the home, on the highway, in traveling, in the factory, on every hand. It is the privilege of every child of God to pray for protection whether in the home, or in traveling on the highway, on a bus, train, or ship. Again, many saints could testify how God has graciously preserved and protected them in answer to prayer.

VI. Praying for Health

All people are dependent on God for life, sustenance, and health. Life originated with God; is sustained by God; therefore, should be lived for God. Our health is a matter of concern with God. Christ made healing a part of His ministry when He was on earth. He can heal us, bless us with good health, renew our youth, and prolong our lives by adding years to them. He said, "I am the Lord that healeth thee" (Ex. 15:26). Since God is concerned about our health and we are concerned about it, we should make it an object of prayer. Some are troubled along the line of praying for health and healing. They wonder, "Should we pray for healing? Is healing in the atonement?" and like questions. To these questions all would have to answer, Yes. We could not place it outside the atonement. In fact, every good thing we have comes not as a result of our own goodness or merits, but as a result of the merits and atoning death of Jesus Christ. All blessings flow from Christ. God will recognize man only through Christ. The mystery of suffering is great, and there are different causes for sickness, such as the sin of the fall, personal sins, the sins of others, malnutrition, contagion, infection, for correction, and because Satan afflicts. The afflicted one should carefully search his heart before God, obey every known commandment, and make it an object of prayer. Dr. R. A. Torrey said that we do not now receive all that has been purchased for us. More will be given to us when Christ comes, at which time we will receive our full redemption. Healing now is only partial and temporary. We now receive healing, renewing, and restoration. We grow old and eventually die; but ultimately, in the resurrection, healing will be complete, final, and perfect. Then the body will be like Christ's body, glorious, immortal, and incorruptible. Since that will be the full redemption, or the complete payment, we now have the "earnest of the inheritance" the down payment, and through Christ have a right and are entitled to a share of it here and now. When we are afflicted or sick, let us take it to the Lord in prayer.

VII. Praying for Employment

It is the will of God that every able person shall be busily employed. This is wholesome and profitable. Be-

ing busily engaged keeps people out of trouble and also
becomes the means for self-preservation and support.
Unemployment has faced good people again and again.
When any Christian is out of employment, it is his
privilege to take it to the Lord in prayer. When God's
children lack work and desire to work, the Lord will
help them to find employment. God has graciously answered prayer for many people and enabled them to
secure employment. Those without employment should
pray about it, assure the Lord of tithes and offerings
and that they will be willing to do any honest work and
do it well without a spirit of striking or boycotting.
Many people could testify that the Lord provided employment for them or led them into an honest business.
When any servant of the Lord has no open door or opportunity for gospel service, God in answer to prayer
can open some door where he may serve Him and
others.

CHAPTER XXX

WHAT TO DO WHEN PRAYERS ARE NOT ANSWERED

It is a great pleasure to receive answers to our prayers. It also is a great pleasure to God to answer our prayers when it glorifies Him and when it is for our good. Every Christian should know to some degree why God answers prayer, and why He does not answer prayer. If our prayers are not answered, there is a reason why they are not answered. When they are not answered, we should not excuse ourselves and say, "Well, it was not God's will to answer our prayer," nor become careless and give up by saying, "It does not matter whether they are answered." The person who will take such a twofold attitude is careless in his prayer life; therefore, will not receive answers to his prayers. This is not the attitude people take when they place an order with a mail-order house. If within a reasonable amount of time they do not receive the order, or an explanation why the goods are not shipped, they do not take the attitude most people do when their prayers are not answered, by saying, "It is not the will of the company to send the goods," or say, "Well, it does not matter whether we receive them." No, indeed not. Of course if the money-order was not included in the order, or the writing was not legible, nor the address given, there would be a just reason why the goods were not received. However, most people are careful when placing an order that the proper amount is included, the right address given, and that the writing is distinct. Then when the goods are not received, and no explanation sent, they write again and enquire why their goods have not been sent. We should be just as vitally concerned, and even more so, when our prayers are not answered, and do something about it.

I. Search Your Own Heart

Never blame God when your prayers are not answered, nor feel that He has not dealt fairly with you. Your own heart needs to be searched, and it should be taken for granted that the reason is at your end of the line and not on the divine side. A search should be made, even as would an electrician after wiring a house and discovering that there was no current in the wires. The trouble would not be with the electricity, or the power house, but with the wiring. The electrician will check every connection and observe whether every law of electricity has been complied with in relation to the lighting of that house. So in the prayer life of the Christian, when his prayers are not answered, he should check over his life, and see that every divine command concerning his life is obeyed and every divine requirement met. If you observe a loose connection, an unmet condition, or an unobserved commandment, these should be met; then God will answer prayer.

II. Ask the Holy Spirit to Search Your Heart

When the electrician can not discover the reason why there is not any current, he will submit the task to an expert electrician. The Christian should not merely trust in his own knowledge, or judgment, and make his own diagnosis why his prayers are not answered, but he should submit his case to the Holy Spirit. The Spirit is the One Who "helpeth our infirmities." What is meant here is our praying infirmities. He helps us in our prayer lives; that is, not only does He help us to pray, but wherein we lack or come short He assists by dictating our requests, inditing our petitions, and in drawing out our pleas. He is greatly concerned about our prayers and that they will be answered. Whenever there are hindering causes, your case should be submitted to the Spirit, for He knows and can reveal to you why your prayers are not answered.

III. See if Christ's Words are Abiding in You

Christ said, "If ye abide in Me, and My words abide in you, ye shall ask what ye will, and it shall be done unto you" (John 15:7). The conditions are "abiding in Christ," and, "His words abiding in you." There is to be a spiritual oneness between Christ and His people. The relation of abiding in Him and His words abiding in you is the source of all your spiritual life and fruitfulness. When His words abide in you and you abide in Him, it secures a oneness, a unity, and a harmony between you and the Lord. This will assure your asking is being endorsed, backed up, and made good by Him. When your prayers are not answered, you should search your heart to see if you are abiding in Him and whether His words are abiding in you.

IV. Delight Yourself in the Lord

The Lord will greatly delight Himself in you if you will delight yourself in Him. He delights in your delights. The promise is, "Delight thyself also in the Lord; and He shall give thee the desires of thine heart" (Ps. 37:4). When your prayers are not answered, you should check on yourself to see if you have been delighting yourself in the Lord. By making God your heart's desire, you will receive your heart's desire. You must delight yourself in God, in His personality, His attributes, His graces, His gifts, and then rest and repose in Him. This will please Him so well that He will see to it that every holy desire will be gratified. Too often people serve the Lord from a subjective viewpoint. Their concern is their own joys, blessings, and pleasures. If these are satisfied, they are pleased. There is a higher, a better way than this, even that of an objective motive, that is, to please the Lord, to glorify Him, to desire to give Him pleasure; then by doing so, you will have your heart's desire.

V. Analyze Your Motives

A self-examination is practical and profitable. When you make a self-examination, the only way to deal with yourself is to be honest and rigid. The Bible commands that you speak to yourself. This also is wholesome. When you do, you have no complaint, no argument to make, and must take it. Praying is such a sacred, serious, and needful task that your motives in it should be to glorify God and to edify others. When there are any selfish motives, they will hinder your prayers from being answered. James, in his Epistle, has something to say about this in these words, "Ye ask, and receive not, because ye ask amiss, that ye may consume it upon your lusts" (James 4:3). Asking for success, plenty, power, and prosperity, or any other things for selfish motives or to consume it on your own lusts, James calls "amiss" asking, and says that is why ye "receive not."

VI. Confess Your Faults

Confession is a potent factor when it comes to obtaining answers to your prayers. Often the hindering element to prayer is some unconfessed sin, mistake, or fault. James writes concerning the prayer of faith which will save the sick, "Confess your faults one to another and pray one for another, that ye may be healed." Too often people do the very opposite of this command, that is, they confess the faults of others and not their own, then forget to pray for them.

VII. Pray Again

Some people say that we should pray for a thing only once, and if we pray for a thing more than once, that implies doubt, or that we did not believe God. This is not so, for if it were, we might ask for so much of certain things that we never would need to ask for them again the rest of our lives. Rather than implying doubt, it implies faith. Bible examples will bear out the truth of this fact. When Elijah prayed for rain and no clouds were observed, he prayed the second time, the third, the fourth, and so on, till he prayed the seventh time. He had faith each time he prayed; that is why he prayed again. Paul mentioned that he prayed daily for certain people and churches. The reason he prayed daily was because he had faith. Some people may contend that asking for a thing more than once becomes vain repetitions, but this should not be considered as such. Christ prayed for the same thing three times, and certainly no person would dare to brand that as "vain repetitions." Neither should we consider the last six prayers that Elijah offered for rain as "vain repetitions." Certainly the thing to do when your prayers are not answered is to pray again.

CHAPTER XXXI

ELIMINATING HINDERING ELEMENTS TO PRAYER

"I press toward the mark for the prize of the high calling of God in Christ Jesus" (Phil. 3:14).

This text does not bear directly on the subject of prayer, but indirectly it does. To press means to push ahead, and to push things aside that crowd into our pathway which retard our spiritual progress. In order to be victorious and successful in the Christian life on earth, and to win the overcomer's crown, every Christian needs to pray much. Prayer is like a tender plant which needs to be set in good soil, then taken care of by cultivating the soil. There are many other seeds which will come up, and these must be weeded out. Many things crowd in on the Christian to crowd out his prayer life, and these need to be pushed to one side to allow passage for a fuller prayer life. Satan will not allow the prayer life of a Christian to go unchallenged, but will hinder in many different ways. It requires pressing to keep up a consistent life of prayer.

I. Inconveniences

There are always some things which will give us trouble or uneasiness in our prayer lives. One is no privacy. Sometimes an evangelist may be so situated in a home with others in his room that it will rob him of privacy and hinder him in praying. To be at our best in prayer, there need to be daily periods when we are alone with the Lord. Other inconveniences may be that of being in a room in which it is too cold to be comfortable, or too hot, a place where flies or mosquitoes pester, etc. Christ had inconveniences. He removed them, or made His own conveniences. We should do as

He did, that is, create conveniences. The urgency of prayer demands that in some manner we create a convenience for prayer.

II. A Lack of Time

This is the case in many lives. Too many excuse themselves from praying by saying they are too busy and do not have time to pray. If any are doing so much that they do not have time to pray, they are doing more than God wants them to do. We need to do as Christ did, that is, make or take time to pray. Sometimes He arose a great while before day to pray (Mark 1:35, 36). In the morning is a good time to pray because it gives time, and God will be given first place. It is seeking the kingdom of God and His righteousness first. In the morning the soul will be more free to pray and the body rested, and the world then is more silent. It was when Christ arose early to be alone, to seek God, to invoke the blessing of God on His ministry, that all men sought Him. The more we seek God and His blessing, the more others will seek our help and contacts. If necessary, ask God for getting-up grace to find time to pray.

III. Social Contacts

The social life has its place and time, but too often others get in our way, or make too many demands upon our time. Too much visiting and contact with others will hinder or rob us of prayer. Christ was thronged many times. What did He do? He left the crowds or dismissed them. On one occasion He sent the multitude away and His disciples across the sea so that He could be alone. Then He went up on a mountain to pray. He prayed the major part of the night, then started on His way to meet them. They were toiling on the sea, having gone about half way, when He overtook them. When they accepted Him on board, immediately the ship arrived at the shore. By praying much during the night He made better progress in a moment than the disciples did in nine hours. By praying more, we too will accomplish much more.

IV. Natural Barriers

While we are in the flesh, we will be beset with natural barriers. There are times when we do not feel like praying, when we are very tired or sleepy. Temptations, or thoughts, may present themselves to us that we are not gifted in praying. Little concern may be felt at times for a concern, or soul burden, or the progress of the cause of Christ. The thing to do is to pray from a sense of duty as well as of responsibility, to stay on our knees before the Lord in prayer until a burden or concern comes to our soul, even if this requires half an hour or more, to assume a concern, to seek a spirit of prayer, and to stir ourselves into action until a burden comes, and we have continued to watch and pray an hour with Him.

V. Mind Wanderings

Who has not been troubled along this line? How often when we have gone into the secret closet to pray, have our minds wandered, and one hundred and one other things have crowded into our thinking and choked out much praying time! It is strange how many things which seem to demand immediate attention will present themselves to us when we are in communion with God. Satan has a way of getting into our thinking and controlling our minds to some extent. When we pray, many other voices and suggestions crowd in to divert our hearts and minds from communion with God. We must battle against this and concentrate our minds on God and close them to all other voices and demands. This involves the exercise of the will, mind, and heart.

VI. Carelessness

Carelessness and neglect act as thieves to rob us of prayer. If we could but realize that prayer is one of the mightiest weapons which God has given us to battle against sin and the forces of Satan, we would shudder at the thought of allowing this weapon to become rusty by misuse. We need to reason along this line and consider what may be accomplished through prayer, and the great things which never come to pass because of a lack of prayer, so that it will stir us into action and a consistent prayer life. Use this weapon, and keep it bright and shining by constant use.

VII. Legitimate Duties

The legitimate duties, or the cares of this life, have crowded the good seed out of many lives. So have legitimate things crowded prayer out of many lives. Business has its place and time, but if we allow business, material things, and the things of time and this world to crowd prayer out, we are neglecting the heavenly, the spiritual, and the eternal things, which are as far superior over the present and material things as eternity is longer than time. Allowing legitimate things to crowd prayer out of our lives will prove disastrous and fatal to the soul.

Let it become a settled fact in our lives that we have time to pray. God gives us time, and it is up to us to take time and utilize it in prayer.

CHAPTER XXXII

EXAMPLES OF THE MINISTRY OF INTERCESSION

Many gifts have been given by the Holy Spirit to people who do not utilize or exercise them. They are laid aside even as the man who was given one talent hid it in the earth, or the man who was given a pound and told to occupy until the giver returned from his far journey kept it laid up in a napkin. Both men allowed that which had been given to them to be unused. Gifts should not be neglected or left unused, but they should be exercised, stirred up, improved, and utilized. By their use they will increase even as the man who had one pound given to him traded in business and gained ten pounds. Another increased his pound fivefold. The ministry of intercession is a great gift. This gift is neglected as much or more than any other gift. Frequently some saints are met who possess the gift of intercession and improve it. It is blessed to meet such characters.

I. Anna the Prophetess Prayed Night and Day

This godly woman lived in Jerusalem in the days of the birth of Christ. Anna was of the tribe of Asher, and of a great age. We do not know exactly how old she was. It is stated, "she was of a great age," that "she was a widow of about fourscore and four years," and that she had lived with her husband seven years before he died. From this we are led to believe she was considerably over a hundred years of age. The important thing about her was she devoted her time in the Lord's house, fasting, praying night and day, praising God, and testifying to all who looked for redemption in Israel. She possessed the ministry of intercession. This was a great ministry for an aged person, and she exercised it to the fullest extent. The reason the Spirit gave us the years of her widowhood (eighty-four) is she spent those years praying. This woman was so aged that evidently her teeth were gone, her hair white, her face wrinkled, her vision nearly gone, and her muscles atrophied. She was too frail and aged to do much work, therefore, she could eat and sleep but little. Since her mind was active and her heart full of the blessing of the Lord, she spent most of her time night and day in prayer. This was a profitable manner in which to invest her time. Many good people are old and can do but little, eat little, and sleep little. Some wish they could decease and be at rest in the Lord. These should not desire to die too soon, for when they get to heaven it will be for ever. They should also remember that after they get to heaven, their ministry will be over, and they can not pray any more for the needy on earth. If only these aged saints of God would make use of the ministry of intercession, each could be worth as much as any active and aggressive minister or missionary. The way in which this may be done is by sitting in an easy chair, rocking while time passes by, or by reclining on a cot, then taking a pastor, an evangelist, or a missionary on his heart, and pray many hours a day for him, and an hour, or several hours, at night when sleep has departed. That pastor, evangelist, or missionary might with five to ten hours of earnest praying for him in every twenty-four become two or three times as fruitful as formerly. He might be surprised at his success, and be constrained to acknowledge his success is due to the prayers of some one else. In this manner every aged saint could be fruitful in old age. We would recommend the example of Anna to every aged person. There is great need for such a ministry. The prayers of an aged saint who was converted early in life, having been faithful all through his or her life and attained maturity will have great weight before God when they are offered in behalf of another. God can well afford

to allow such saints who exercise the ministry of intercession to live to an old age. Many dear saints of God,
because of age and infirmities, have retired and are
physically superannuated. These could become spiritually aggressive and live lives of intercession which
would bless and influence multitudes for good. Certainly the prayers of an aged saint will have a greater
weight with God than the prayers of a novice. The
prayers of a mature saint are loaded with maturity,
faith, fidelity, wisdom, experience, an acquired holiness,
and a heavenliness which give them weight, even as
a heavily loaded truck when it has attained a high
speed; the momentum carries it on and powerful brakes
are needed to bring it to a full stop. If aged people
could see their privilege along this line, their declining
years could be a great blessing and they could bear
fruit in old age.

II. Two Women Who Prayed for D. L. Moody

D. L. Moody was being greatly used of God, but he
felt there were much greater things in store for him.
He realized more and more how little he was fitted by
personal acquirements for his work, and how much he
needed to be qualified for service by the Holy Spirit's
power. This realization was deepened by conversations
with two women who sat on the front pew in his church.
From the expression of their faces he could see they
were praying. At the close of the service, they would
say to him, "We have been praying for you."

"Why don't you pray for the people?" Mr. Moody
would ask.

"Because you need the power of the Spirit," was
their reply.

"I need the power! Why?" said he in relating the
incident afterwards, "I thought I had power. I had
the greatest congregation in Chicago, and there were
many conversions. I was in a sense satisfied. But right
along those two godly women kept praying for me, and

their earnest talk about anointing for special service set me thinking. I asked them to come and talk with me, and they poured out their hearts in prayer that I might receive the filling of the Spirit. There came a great hunger in my soul. I did not know what it was. I began to cry out as I never did before. I really felt that I did not want to live if I could not have this power for service." During this period in which he hungered for a deeper experience, Chicago was laid in ashes. Mr. Moody went east to New York City to collect funds for the sufferers from the Chicago fire and to rebuild his church, but while there his heart was crying out for power from on high. "My heart was not in the work of begging," said he. "I was crying all the time that God would fill me with His Spirit. Well, one day in the city of New York—oh, what a day!—I cannot describe it; I seldom refer to it; it is almost too sacred an experience to name; . . . I went to preaching again. The sermons were not different; I did not present any new truths; and yet hundreds were converted. I would not now be placed back where I was before that blessed experience if you should give me all the world. It would be as the small dust of the balance." What a blessing it would be if more godly people who possess a measure of discernment could discern that some young workers should be filled with the Spirit, and pray for them daily until they receive such a baptism and outpouring of the Spirit which would qualify and capacitate them for a greater ministry! Those two women who prayed for Mr. Moody until he received his Spirit baptism performed a great ministry.

III. A Mother of Israel in Her Seventies

It is essential to be filled with the Spirit to live a life of prayer. Dr. S. A. Keen relates that he and another Christian brother went to visit a mother of Israel. She was up in her seventies, and was a veritable Doctor of Divinity, and more truely entitled to that degree than many who bear it. She had walked, talked, and lived with God so long that she had a wonderful insight into divine and spiritual things. After a season of prayer she recited the story of her Christian life; how, when a girl in her teens, she was converted, and at once began to pray for her youthful associates, and saw many of them converted. Later she married a Methodist class-leader and their home became the meeting place of a weekly prayer meeting. Here she saw many converted and fully sanctified. Then she said, "I have been the mother of twelve children, all of whom were converted while I was praying with and for them. Now, brother," she said, addressing her pastor, "I am feeble, and can not get to the house of God, but every Sabbath morning when the bell rings for public worship, I begin to pray for you and your message, and for the people, and I continue to pray until I think the service is over. So I do when the prayer meeting comes around." Then she spoke of a young man, a neighbor's son, for whom she was praying. "There is also our physician just across the street; I am asking God to save him: he is a skeptic." What a beautiful life for an aged lady to live! What a life of usefulness she was living in her old age when most aged people give up doing good and live a good passive life! She started in her teens and for over sixty years without a break enjoyed a ministry of intercession.

IV. Invalid Woman in England Prayed for Arrival of Moody

Invalid people should not despair of doing good or give themselves over to fate by doing nothing for the Lord. Many who are invalids have clear minds which are active, and thoughts pass through them all day. Since they can not work, why could not these employ their hearts and minds by getting in touch with God and exercise the ministry of intercession? They could pray hours every day; then in answer to their prayers, God would richly bless the ministry of others. This fact is illustrated by G. Campbell Morgan of England, who said he had an invalid woman in his congregation who prayed down revivals for D. L. Moody. She had read of Moody and his revivals in America. Then she prayed, "O Lord, send Dwight L. Moody to our church and give us a revival." God was working at that end of the line. She prayed daily for over a year. God began to work in answer to her prayers at the other end of the line. He moved D. L. Moody to go to England without any call from man. His personal desire was to learn the art of preaching from the great preachers in England. However, God designed that he should be used in revival meetings there, and to honor the prayers and faith of this invalid woman. When Moody arrived, he went into the church of G. Campbell Morgan, who insisted that he preach. Moody preached and the service was only ordinary. The invalid's sister was there and heard Moody. She came home and said, "Who do you think preached in our church today? Make a guess." She made a few guesses, then said she did not know. Then her sister told her, "Dwight L. Moody from America." It almost took her breath. "O," said she, "do not bring me any dinner; neither allow any visitors to come into my room, for I want to be left alone." She was encouraged and thrilled that God had answered her prayers by sending Moody to her church. Now she wanted to give herself to prayer that God would send a revival. That evening Moody preached again. He said the spiritual atmosphere was only common, but the longer he preached the greater became the inspiration and blessing which fell on him. When he was through he made his appeal by saying all who desired to become Christians should stand. Instantly five hundred people sprang to their feet. Moody was surprised, and thought the people in England stood out of courtesy; therefore, he told every one to sit down. He made the proposition a little stronger, and again asked those who wanted to accept Christ as their Savior to stand. Again five hundred people stood. Still thinking they did not understand him, he said all should sit down. He tried to make more clear what he meant; then he said, "All who want to accept Christ pass into the inquiry room." Immediately, five hundred people streamed into the

inquiry room. Mr. Moody seemed shocked. He said, "I
have never seen anything in this fashion." When he re-
covered himself, he said, "Somebody has been praying
around here. Who has been praying?" He was informed
about this invalid lady. He said, "I must see that person." The next day he was taken to see this praying
woman. Moody gave her a new Bible and wrote his
name in it. She said, "I'll pray for you every day as
long as I will live." The beauty of her prayer life was
she lived longer than Moody. God could afford to allow her to live long, even though she was an invalid,
to pray for His servant, Moody. When Moody died, she
said to her pastor, "Dr. Morgan, I'll pray for you just as
I prayed for Moody." This woman prayed down a revival. There are many other women who could do the
same in their communities if they would live lives of
faith and intercession.

V. Two Godly Women Prayed for a Revival

Several years ago two godly women in the southern
part of the state of Indiana became greatly burdened
that a revival meeting should come to their community.
A generation was growing up around them which had
not been influenced by a revival meeting. These two
women prayed for two years that God would send a
revival to their community. God answered their prayers
by sending two young preachers who were just start-
ing out in the ministry, neither one having had one
year's experience in the ministry. They pitched a tent
in that community and preached to the people. Feeble
as their efforts were, God greatly honored their ministry and in a gracious manner answered the prayers
of those two godly women. One hundred thirteen people were definitely converted. These were not cold
church members and backsliders warmed over, but
people who had not been converted before. This revival also resulted in a church being built in the community, and seventy-five out of this number united with
the church. That church is thriving today. Since two
women in one community prayed down a gracious re-

vival, why could this not be duplicated in many other communities? Certainly God would like to send gracious revivals into many communities. If two or three godly people would agree, and meet together frequently, say once or twice a week, and pray earnestly for a revival, keeping it up for a year or two, or even longer if necessary, in due time God would answer prayer and send a revival.

VI. A Pastoral Body Prayed for Their Pastor

The Bethany Presbyterian Church in Philadelphia had secured Dr. J. Wilbur Chapman as their pastor. Mr. John Wanamaker, that great Sunday School leader and worker, was an official of the pastoral committee. He had gone to London to hear Charles H. Spurgeon preach, to observe his work, and to learn from him. He came home and related to his pastor, Dr. Chapman, that he discovered the secret of Spurgeon's great power and success. When Dr. Chapman asked John Wanamaker what the secret of his success was, he said that Dr. Spurgeon's church officials prayed with him, sat near him, and cheered him as he stood pleading with the people. This pastor suggested that his church officials should do the same for him, which they readily agreed to do. Dr. Chapman wrote that sometimes as many as twenty-four of them sat on the platform, which gave him but little space in which to move. Being near them as he moved about, he would hear an elder say, "Amen." Then another would whisper, "God bless you." He would sometimes get on the side where Mr. Wanamaker sat and hear him say, "That is splendid! God bless you." Sometimes Mr. Wanamaker would rub his hand up and down his pastor's arm in a manner which was greatly appreciated. What inspiring acts for church officials to do to help, encourage, and inspire their pastor!

Most churches relax, fail to pray for their pastor, and think he should do it all. They say, "Well, that is why we have hired him, and we pay him a salary to do the praying and to pull the holy fire down on us." Yes, and if he does well, they consider he is paid for it and has just done his duty; but if he does not do well, they say, "He is of little value," and set him aside. It is the privilege of every pastoral committee to be so spiritual, to pray so much for their pastor until he will be set on fire; then he will set the entire church on fire. Let more churches follow this policy, that is, faithfully, unitedly, consistently, and persistently pray for their pastor; then God will honor their prayers, bless their pastor, and the entire church will prosper.

VII. Two Hundred Members Prayed for Their Pastor

The praying power of a spiritual church, when developed to its highest efficiency, is tremendous. Not many churches live up to their prayer privileges and possibilities. The church in which the prayer possibilities are developed will be teeming with spiritual life, growth, revival fires, missionary zeal; and the streams of blessing will flow because the channel, both in its intake and its outlet, is open. Charles H. Spurgeon was pastor of such a church. His tabernacle work was blessed and many were converted. A goodly number entered the ministry. The activities of his great church gave expression along different lines of Christian work. One time a person asked Spurgeon the question, "What is the secret of your success?" He replied, "My people pray for me." Each Sunday evening, one hour preceding the evening service, two hundred people gathered in the basement of his tabernacle to pray for him. Two hundred people praying one hour is equivalent to one man praying two hundred hours. Consider, two hundred hours of prayer back of one sermon! Such a sermon preached by a man of God would be greatly blessed by God.

A young minister went to London to visit C. H. Spurgeon and learn from him. At the close of a day of blessing and success in the tabernacle, he tried to thank Spurgeon; but the elderly minister replied, "Tut, tut, my brother, the blessing is from above. Every day and night thousands in the English speaking world are praying for the tabernacle and for me as the pastor. If you wish to have a soul-winning church, get your people to pray."

There is great virtue in continued and repeated praying for one thing by one individual. There is great virtue in united praying, in which two or three agree and continue to pray for one thing until it comes to pass. Christ has given us promises which encourage individual and collective praying. The ministry of intercession could be exercised by many Christians if they would give themselves to prayer. These intercessors would help to "make up the hedge and stand in the gap before the Lord," which would move God to give favor, victory, and success to His servants and their service.

CHAPTER XXXIII

THE RESULTS OF TRUE WORSHIP

The supreme thing a Christian can do in the sight of God is to worship Him. The Father seeks worshipers. The Son of God seeks sinners; and the Holy Spirit seeks pupils and believers whom He may cleanse, fill, empower, lead, and teach. There is very little true worship offered to God by men. It is natural for all men to worship something. No sin is as provocative and insulting to God as idolatry. No sin is as degrading and demoralizing to man as the sin of idolatry. Idolatry is the sin of abomination which brings desolation. On the other hand, no act of man is more pleasing to God, and more gratifying to man, than worshiping the heavenly Father.

I. What Worship is Not

Many people do not know what true worship is. The word "worship" is used in a very loose manner. We often hear the expressions, "The Morning Worship Service," "The Evening Worship Service," "Let Us Worship the Lord in Singing," or "Let Us Worship the Lord in Prayer." Bible reading is not worship, but it is reading what God has said. Meditation is not worship, but it is thinking on the goodness of God and taking time to digest and assimilate the Word of God. Listening to a sermon is not worship. That is hearing what the minister has to say about God and the Bible. Giving thanks is not worship. Thanksgiving is offering gratitude to God and expressing our appreciation for His blessings which He has given us. Singing is not worship. Singing is making a joyful, harmonious noise which expresses our good inward feelings. Praying is not worship. Praying is talking to God, even asking for His help, or blessings for ourselves or for some one else. These acts may and should lead to worshiping God, and they may and should contain an element of worship, but in themselves they are not worship. These things are mostly subjective and manward, in which we are taken up with our needs, our joys, etc.

II. What True Worship Is

We read frequently in the Bible that, "they bowed their heads and worshiped," "they bowed their faces to the earth and worshiped," "they fell on their faces and worshiped," and like expressions. Worship is objective, it is Godward. Worship is being taken up with God, not ourselves. Worship is the soul bowing in loving adoration to God and with willing submission to Him, in which there is an inward urge surging Godward in which He is contemplated, loved, and adored. Worship is being taken up only with God.

III. Whom to Worship

God and God alone is the object of worship. Men, saints, angels, and money are not objects of worship. To worship any one or anything beside God is idolatry. We may admire men, but we do not adore or worship them. Worshiping any one else, or anything else, not only is idolatry, but it is robbing God of His dues. Christ said, "Thou shalt worship the Lord thy God, and Him only shalt thou serve" (Matt. 4:10). Christ also said, "True worshipers shall worship the Father in spirit and in truth" (John 4:23). We should worship the Father. The writer to the Hebrews said, "When He bringeth in the firstbegotten into the world, He saith, And let all the angels of God worship Him" (Heb. 1:6). Christ, the Son of God, is an object of worship, and men and angels are commanded by God to worship Him (Phil. 2:10, 11). Then the Holy Ghost, Who also is God, is an object of worship. He is to be loved and adored.

IV. Our Duty to Worship God

We owe worship to God because He is the supreme

Being in the universe, because of Who He is and what He does. We owe worship to Christ because He is our Creator and Redeemer, and because the Father commands it. It is our first duty to Him. It is not enough to believe Him, obey Him, pray to Him, praise Him, give to Him, but also to worship Him. God desires all of these, but He seeks worshipers. First of all, we are saved to worship Him, then to serve Him. Worship is more pleasing to Him than anything else. Satan is aware of this fact. He will offer a higher price for it than anything else. Satan offered Christ the whole world and all the kingdoms if He would fall down and worship him.

V. Where to Worship God

In the Old Testament period, God designated Jerusalem as the place His people were to go to worship Him. The Samaritans claimed that Mount Gerizim was the place to worship God, and the Jews claimed that Jerusalem was the only place set apart by God to worship. When Christ was on earth, He said that the hour was coming when neither in Mount Gerizim nor in Jerusalem the Father was to be worshiped. Then Christ informed us that even then the hour had come that the Father was to be worshiped in spirit and in truth. The Samaritans did not worship in truth. Their worship was corrupted. The Jews did not worship in spirit, for their worship had become formal, cold, and dry. They did not accept the Son of God; therefore, the Father in heaven did not accept their formal ceremonies. It is not so much the place of worship that counts, but it is the state of the heart in which we worship that pleases the Father. People do not need to go to Jerusalem to worship; they may worship God any where in the world.

VI. How to Worship God

It often is expressed that prayer is a blood-bought privilege. This is true of worshiping God. In Old Testament periods when any one approached God, it was through sacrifice, through the death of an innocent victim and substitute. No person was allowed to loaf around the courts of the tabernacle or saunter into the courts of the Lord. The person who did so was to be killed. It required the death of an innocent and perfect victim to enter into the courts. The same was true concerning the high priest's entrance into the most holy place for all Israel. He could enter in only with blood. After all sins and sin had been atoned for by a trespass offering and a sin offering, only then could an Israelite offer a meat offering (meal offering which was bloodless and typified works). The peace offering and the burnt offering, which in some aspects typified worship, were to be offered freely by the people. These also were blood offerings. Even so, our approach unto the Father, whether in seeking salvation or in behalf of others or in worship, can only be on the ground of the shed-blood of Christ. Therefore, the way to worship the Father is; (1) On the ground of the shed-blood of Christ, or as the writer to the Hebrews expresses it, "enter into the holiest by the blood of Christ" (Heb. 10:19). We should come to God in prayer and in worship on this condition, and also attach the value of the blood of Christ to our worship. This will make it acceptable and valuable to the Father. (2) Then our worship should be by and in the Holy Spirit (Phil. 3:3). That is, the Spirit should direct and inspire our hearts in worship to the Father. He will do so if He dwells in us and we co-operate with Him as He operates. Our worship and all our labors will be accepted by the Father when the Spirit is inspiring them. (3) Our worship should be in the spirit. Christ said, "Worship the Father in spirit," and "God is a Spirit: and they that worship Him must worship Him in spirit" (John 4:23, 24). "In spirit" means the opposite of "in the flesh." The spirit is the inner man. The flesh is the body, or the outer man. It is possible for the head and the body to bow and the heart or spirit not to do so before God. To do so is mere profession or pretense. If it is in the flesh, it will not be accepted by God, for that becomes only a form and is not the real thing, but is dry, and lifeless. Worshiping God "in the spirit" is the heart, the inner man bowing before God, which involves the will, the desires, and the emotions. This is what God seeks, desires, and accepts. (4) Our worship is to be in truth. Christ emphasized this fact. He stated that we must worship "in truth" (John 4:23, 24). In truth means in reality, sincerity, and soundness of belief. A sound belief in God and in His Word is essential to make our worship acceptable to the Father. (5) Then our worship should be offered to God reverently, courageously, and boldly. We are commanded to come to the throne of grace boldly (Heb. 4:16 and 10:19). Not to do so displeases the Lord and disobeys His commands.

VII. The Results of True Worship

The results of true worship are far greater than we realize. The benefits of it, both Godward and manward, are more far-reaching than we can comprehend. (1) True worship satisfies the Father and brings joy to His loving heart. When we offer it unto Him, He has found that which He has sought; then He will rejoice, for this is the one thing above all others that He desires. (2) The worshiper is satisfied and blessed. This will bring more joy and satisfaction to the heart than any thing else can bring. There can be no higher, deeper, fuller, more satisfying, more edifying, purer joy to the heart than that which arises from the soul bowing before God in adoration, contemplation, and submission to Him Who is supreme and seeks worship. (3) True worship empties the worshiper of himself, which makes more room for God to fill him with Himself, with His virtues, and qualities. This is most wholesome and edifying in the Christian life, and brings a rapid spiritual growth. (4) True worship leads the worshiper to become transformed into God's likeness. We become like the object we worship. It is as we tarry in His presence that the image of God becomes impressed on the worshipers. Astronomers photograph the stars by setting the camera with its sensitive negative focused through a powerful telescope to revolve with the heavens, allowing almost a whole night's exposure. When the sensitive plates are developed, faint impressions of other worlds are revealed on the negative which could not be seen with the eye through the telescope. Moses lingered in the presence of a holy God until he imbibed so much of the holiness of God that it gave expression in glory which emanated from him. His face shone so that people could not look on him, which necessitated his wearing a covering over his face while he talked to them.

Have you ever worshiped Him? Do you spend some time each day in worshiping Him? Let us worship the Father because He seeks it. By worshiping Him on earth, we will be better fitted for the service of heaven and eternity. The work of redemption will find its culmination and completion in the redemption and glorification of a people fitted to worship God through eternity. We read, "They shall serve Him day and night in His temple." The word "serve" is translated "worship" elsewhere in the Bible. "O come, let us worship and bow down: let us kneel before the Lord our Maker" (Ps. 95:6).